The Ministry of Restoration

Touching the Hem Of His Garment

Prayer & Devotional Handbook

Shalisa Anthony

Printed and bound in USA by Createspace

ISBN: 1542744989
ISBN-13: 978-1542744980

Dedication

The Ministry of Restoration Prayer and Devotional Book is for everyone who has ever struggled to pray - but never knew where to start.

It starts when you reach out.
Your release, your answer, is in your touch.

This book is for you.

Index

Acknowledgements

To the heart of God, which is ever revealing, calling and stirring....

To the Ministry of Restoration International Pentecostal Church
for responding and caring;

To the following contributors for sharing their hearts and their prayers:
Lisa Anthony-Rigsby,
Alison Agard
Nathalie Byer
Margaret Dyer
Susan McCarthy
Maxine Yearwood-Bailey

Special acknowledgment to Brother Bovell of Ministry of Restoration,
who has waited a long, long, LONG time for this! God bless you!

Introduction

THE TOUCH: *"The smell of stale blood, mixed with the pungent odour of fear, was overpowering. Waves of a tingling sensation flowed up and down her body, from her head to chest, down to her stomach, legs and feet and back up again, wave after wave of this new and pleasant feeling! She stiffened as she felt it concentrate and settle in her womb, the cause of her painful condition. She gasped loudly in shock and surprise as she felt her womb tighten and her stomach rise as the constant, painful and familiar flow between her thighs, throb slowly to a standstill!*

She didn't know what was going on but she knew she had not laughed like that for well, years now. Truth to be told, she did not have much to smile about, much less laugh at. Suddenly, she became aware of a growing silence as the laughter around her started to die down. It was her laughter which was the only sound filling the air, as she rediscovered how to laugh again! She filled the air with a pure sound of joy, love, happiness and release.

The crowd slowly and, so it seem to her, painfully parted to let Him through. As He drew near, the compulsion to kneel at His feet overwhelmed her. She started to talk. Quietly at first. Unbelievingly at first. Trying to make sense of all that had happened, even as she garbled incoherently, hysterically, emotionally. She was healed! He had healed her! She had made it – she didn't miss! Somehow, she was successful! Even though she thought she'd failed, He alone had heard the silent scream of her prayer. It was the sound of her touch, a touch of desperation and faith, which He had caught, even in the midst of a pushing and shoving crowd. Yes, her determination, persistence, patience and perseverance had finally paid off.

Standing above her, He gently reached down and touched her head. Lifting her face to His, His eyes met hers. His face lit up with a smile which seemed to obliterate the sun.

"I knew it was you who had touched Me", He said, in a gentle whisper. "It was the sound of your touch which called out to Me. The virtue in Me responded, and I felt it leave Me, in answer to your need. My daughter, go in peace and live. Your belief and trust made you whole, when your faith reached out to Me".

Outline

The purpose of this book is to help you to reach out in faith (or even fear!), and t dare to touch the hem of His garment. You may not think your prayers have made it past the ceiling. You may even doubt if He will ever hear you – but just reach out! Just reach out! The poems, the prayers, the affirmations have been written by people just like you and me, who are all seeking a touch and a reaction from the Master. We are desperate for an answer, a reply, a response. For we are all in need of mercy, grace, compassion, forgiveness, strength, healing and above all, love.

So … Where Do I Start?

It's very simple. Find a **topic** from the index which best addresses your present situation. Or just open and start right from where you are; it's as simple as that! Each topic has a:

- **Poetry Pause,** designed to give you a creative perspective on the topic.

- **Action Section**, to help direct you to what you need to do in order to move forward. It also prepares you for the next important section –

- **Prayer Section**. Each prayer is to help you construct your own prayer, in your own words, so you can grow and develop your own prayer life.

- **The word from the Word** is a selection of relevant bible verses. Meditate on them and use them to change your thought patterns regarding the issues and problems you may be facing. There's power in The Word! Jesus said "The Words I speak to you, are spirit and life", so actively use this section to feed yourself.

- At the end of each section, is a **"Touching the Hem of His Garment"** segment.

These key points will encourage you to stretch and grow, and to use your faith to touch the One, whose attention you are seeking. Our prayer is that the Master will hear your heart's cry and respond to your outstretched hand. Be assured that the call of your touch will invite Him to minister and answer you, right where you are. So, whoever and wherever you are, welcome to

"Touching the Hem of His Garment Prayer and Devotional Book.

Shalisa Anthony

Shalisa

Ministry of Restoration International
Pentecostal Church, London UK

MOR

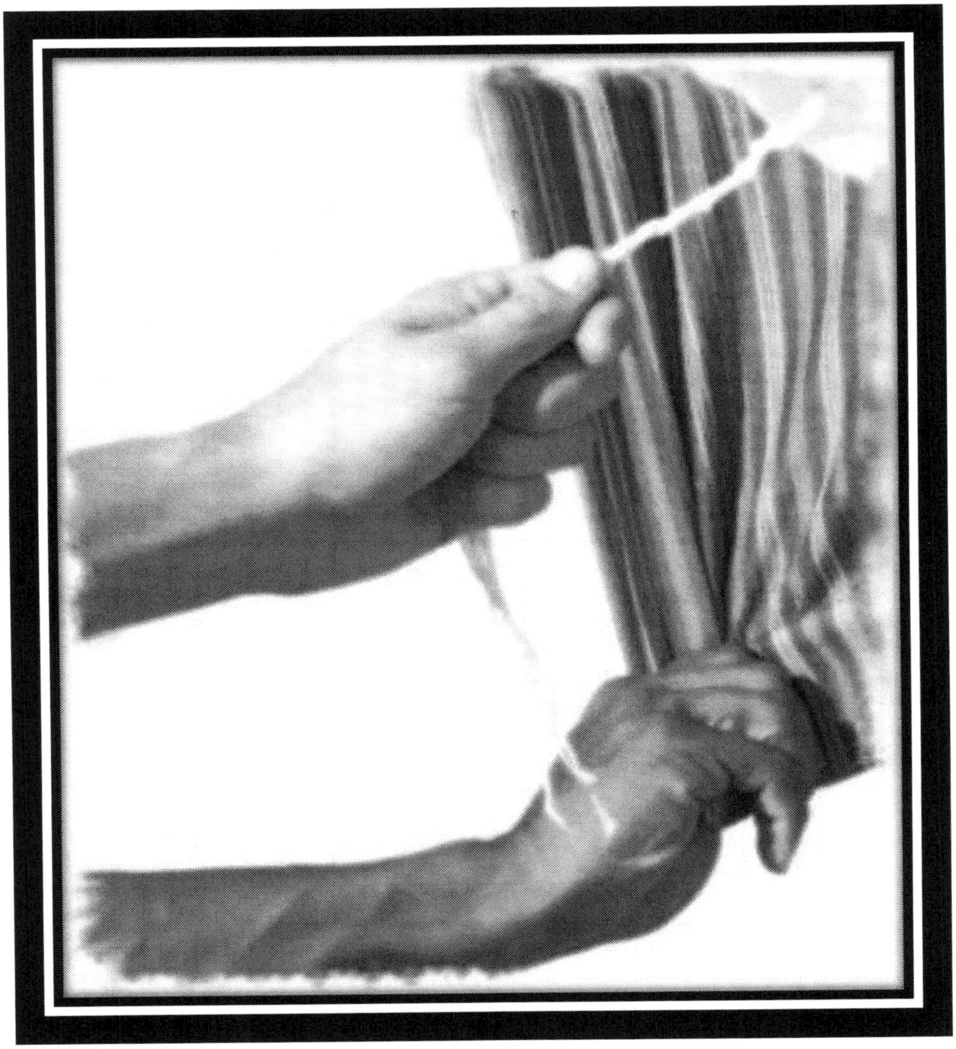

Let your faith touch the hem of His Garment

1 Finances

The term, or notion of "finances", has been around for a long time. It relates to an old term meaning "*to end or ending*", i.e. by satisfying or something that is due. It has its origins in the Greek word "*telos*", which means "*to end*".

From Medieval Latin, "*finis*" grew to mean "*a payment in settlement, fine or tax*" and by the 14th century, the term "*finance*" it had evolved to its current meaning, based on a Middle French expression to "*end, ending or settlement of a debt.*"

So, if the above definition of finance implies an end or settlement, then why, oh why, do we never seem to have enough of it? Why is money the major cause of so much stress and worry? Like an elusive lover, it entices us with promises beyond our wildest dreams, which we think would all be met - if we could only get close enough to touch it, have it and hold it! Sadly, for many of us, money never seems to deliver on its covert promises when we do eventually, manage to get a little bit closer, to having just a little bit more, in order to go a little bit further.

This section is to share a little of what God says about finance, money and all that jazz! You may not get rich overnight but you will get peace of mind and, to be honest - that is definitely something money cannot buy! It's time to tap into the real wealth and riches of life. It's time to touch the hem of His garment for a financial release.

FINANCIAL BLESSINGS

Makes you blessed to be a blessing

Money, You Said...

You said you'd be there for me
And I believed you.
You made me pursue you and yearn for you
Cos I believed you.

Like your name "Currency", you flowed in and out of my life
And I tried to surfboard on you
But you let me down.
You ebbed in and out, like an elusive midsummer tide
And left me with the flotsam and seaweed of debt and broken pride...

Yet, the Word says that "money answers all things"
Could it be that I'm asking the wrong questions?
Seeking for my circumstances, the wrong solutions?

Yes finances, money, cash, wonga, dosh –
Whatever alias you're using now
You said you'd be there for me – and like a fool, I still believed you
But in paying off my dues with a broken heart and furrowed brow
I wonder, who's paying off who...?

Lisa Anthony-Rigsby

Party for Laughter, Wine for happiness
MONEY IS FOR EVERYTHING!

I Quit...

I finally quit my financial overlords
Big Daddy Visa and Master-Card!
Too long they've held me captive
And worked me long and hard!

Yep, today I dropped my oh, so plastic friends
Who promised me the world and so much more
Only to find myself at a financial dead-end
After taking many a spending spree detour!

I feel so light and free to just be me
And to pay for what I need!
At last I'm beginning to understand
The importance of money being a "seed"

And begin to sow where it's needed most
In the lives of people and not just in things;
For whilst money can buy you diamonds and pearls,
It's got no power to cleanse you within!

So yes folks, I quit the money train,
The slaving after the paper chain;
I quit so that I can now live free
And begin to work so that money will now run after me...!

Lisa Anthony-Rigsby

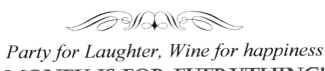

You need an answer – and you need it NOW! You need money to help you make ends meet. (In fact, you need money to help you find the ends!) You finances, because you want to help someone else to get out of their own pit of financial demise. We will all come to a point in life when, after we have exhausted family, friends and credit cards, we can only turn to God for a financial blessing to get out of debt, to provide the basic necessities for our families, or even to pay the light bill. If this describes your current situation or life circumstances, do not despair. This is YOUR time for action!

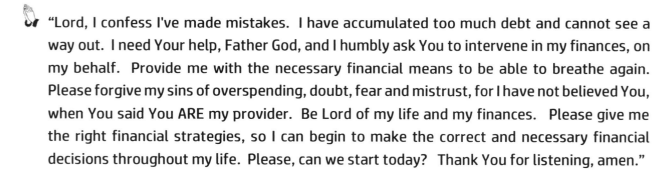

"Heavenly Father, I come before you today to ask for a financial blessing to improve my life. My faith keeps me strong, and I know you will provide for me and the people I love. I do not seek a large sum of money. I do not trouble you for unneeded comforts or luxury. I only ask for enough money to relieve my financial woes and ease this stress. Give me the means to do Your work and spread Your love. Father, You know my heart and my desire to be a blessing. There is so much I want to do and to give, and I humbly ask to be given a chance. Thank You for hearing me. Amen"

"Lord, I confess I've made mistakes. I have accumulated too much debt and cannot see a way out. I need Your help, Father God, and I humbly ask You to intervene in my finances, on my behalf. Provide me with the necessary financial means to be able to breathe again. Please forgive my sins of overspending, doubt, fear and mistrust, for I have not believed You, when You said You ARE my provider. Be Lord of my life and my finances. Please give me the right financial strategies, so I can begin to make the correct and necessary financial decisions throughout my life. Please, can we start today? Thank You for listening, amen."

"Lord, I panic when I hear and read about the current economic situation. I worry about how my family and I will cope. Without my income and my job, I don't know how I will manage. I know I should trust You, but my faith is small and my fear is large. Work with me and help me to keep my focus on You, the Source of all my income. I know that without You, money is meaningless, as it cannot buy love, life, happiness or health. I believe You will meet my needs, because in Your Word, You promised You would. So, based on what YOU have said, I place my faltering faith and trembling trust in You. It's time for me to trust You, to supply my every need. I'm reaching out; please touch back! Amen!"

Do not toil to acquire wealth; be discerning enough to desist. When your eyes light on it, it is gone, for suddenly it sprouts wings, flying like an eagle toward heaven. Proverbs 23:4-5

🕮 *An Invitation to Abundant Life:* "Ho! Everyone who thirsts, come to the waters; and you who have no money, come, buy and eat! Yes, come, buy wine and milk without money and without price! *Isaiah 55:1*

🕮 But those who desire to be rich fall into temptation and a snare, and into many foolish and harmful lusts which drown men in destruction and perdition. For the **love** of money is a root of all kinds of evil, for which some have strayed from the faith in their greediness, and pierced themselves through with many sorrows. But you, O man of God, flee these things and pursue righteousness, godliness, faith, love, patience, gentleness. *1 Timothy 6:10*

Finance is a tool to help meet your dreams

DON'T DREAM ABOUT FINANCE

Time to Touch: Finances

If you have been viewing money as the source, instead of a resource, this is a timely reminder to shift your focus on **the** Source of all good things, and begin to look to Him to provide your needs.

So all you have to do is:

- ★ Open your hands outward and upward.
- ★ Look up.
- ★ Take a deep breath in. exhale (*repeat twice or as many times as you feel necessary*)
- ★ Now, when you feel ready, simply ask The Source, God, to bring to you what you **need** financially, right where you are...and just believe

It is important to believe when you pray. If you think it can't, won't or will never happen, why not flip the script? It's time to change the tape in your mind, time to change what you say and choose to believe. Take a breath and dare to reach out to believe God can and will hear your prayers. What have you got to lose?

2 Favour

Favour is generally defined as:

- *friendly or well-disposed regard; goodwill*
- *the state of being approved or held in regard:*
- *excessive kindness or unfair partiality; (unmerited) preferential treatment:*

Or to put it another way, favour is...

- ✯ When doors which have been closed to others, suddenly open up – *just for you.*
- ✯ When the train is full and the guard allows you to ride in the special compartment reserved for staff – *just for you.*
- ✯ When you are suddenly plucked from the midst of obscurity into the spotlight of opportunity – and it happened, *just for you*!
- ✯ When a special item you'd had your eye on is not only reduced, but you get an additional discount when you go to pay! Now THAT is favour!

Favour shows up in so many ways in our lives – but the problem is we don't always recognise it as such. We call it luck, fortune and a number of other words. Favour is simply a loving God smiling on His favourite child – YOU!

The Word says, when a man is at peace with God, even his enemies favour him, as the righteous (the believer) is surrounded by a shield of favour (***Proverbs 16:7***). It means your enemies will have a "friendly or well-disposed regard" towards you. Indeed, once you live a life in, with and for God, you can expect excessive kindness, unfair partiality and abundant goodwill to come your way. (Others looking on may think it "unfair", but with God, it is simply favour!) So begin to declare, believe and expect that preferential treatment - FAVOUR - is yours! Because what others may consider as unfair, when things start to positively turn around for you, is simply your time and turn to be favoured!

Starting today, you can choose to operate and walk in favour, goodwill, approval and regard. Simply decide to change your mind-set and start to claim the promises in the Word of God for yourself. As you read this section, I sincerely pray the "favour" of God will become a tangible reality in your life, today and every day!

Favour Me!

"Favour me, don't ignore or overlook me!"

It's time for life to begin to change for the best!
It's time for life to single me out from all the rest!
It's time for life to give me that special chance;
To change the beat so I can now sing and dance!

Surely it's time for life to lower the bar,
To give me a chance to extend and run far!
A chance for me to leapfrog my limit to reach the sky
And get a chance to spread my wings and fly!

So I'm on the lookout for favour when it comes!
It's got my address details, it's knows my home.
Favour is impartial and does not have favourites;
All I have to do is prepare and get ready to meet it!

Lisa Anthony-Rigsby

IT'S NEVER LUCK

It's always God's favour!

...I Asked For...

I asked for *strength*... and God gave me difficulties to make me strong.
I asked for *wisdom*... and God gave me problems to solve
I asked for *prosperity*... and God gave me brawn and brain to work.
I asked for *courage*... and God gave me dangers to overcome.
I asked for *patience*...and God placed me in situations where I was forced to wait.
I asked for *love*... and God gave me troubled people to help.
I asked for *favours*... and God gave me opportunities.
I received *nothing* I wanted.   I received ***everything*** I needed.
MY PRAYERS HAVE BEEN ANSWERED.

Nathalie Byer

You may need a prayer for favour and for God to move on your behalf. But **you** need to be ready to receive the change, elevation and turnaround God has been waiting to give you! Ready? Are you sure? Then let's go – it's action time!

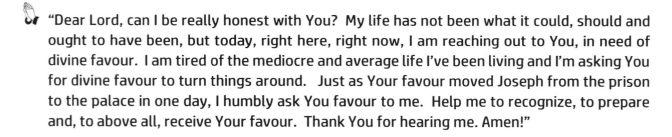

"Dear Father, thank you for another wonderful day! I confess I do not know what the day may hold, but I do know that You hold today, every day and all my days, in Your hands. I have decided to trust You and, based on Your word towards me, today I declare that I walk in Your favour. I boldly declare I am strong and well able to fulfill my God given destiny. I declare I am a victor and not a victim. I may have been defeated before, but the past is past. This is a new day, and my time to walk in divine favour! Thank You, Lord, Amen!"

"Dear Lord, can I be really honest with You? My life has not been what it could, should and ought to have been, but today, right here, right now, I am reaching out to You, in need of divine favour. I am tired of the mediocre and average life I've been living and I'm asking You for divine favour to turn things around. Just as Your favour moved Joseph from the prison to the palace in one day, I humbly ask You favour to me. Help me to recognize, to prepare and, to above all, receive Your favour. Thank You for hearing me. Amen!"

"Father, Your Word says the righteous shall receive favour from their enemies, because You will surround them as with a shield of favour. That means all which pertains to me – work, family, finances, health, business, everything – is now surrounded by Your favour! Therefore, Father, I claim Your favour to deal with (*name your situation and circumstances* ______________). Based on Your Word, I declare and decree Your favour over this situation. I believe it has already come to pass in heaven and I await the manifestation of it, here on earth, for Your glory. I claim divine and exceptional favour in Christ Jesus' Name! Oh Father, I thank You for having heard and granted my prayer for more of Your favour in my life. Thank You, in Jesus' name. Amen."

"It does not seem fair, when I see others moving forward, faster and further along their path, than where I am. It really hurts and I can't help but wonder, why am I so unfortunate? Why has life dealt me such an unfavourable hand? Forgive me for being so envious of others for the favour You give them! It's not easy but I need Your help. So help me to wait and to be ready for my turnaround when it comes! Because You are not a partial God, I believe and know that divine favour is also my portion. So just hold my hand and lead, guide and direct me, so I may walk today and every day, in Your favour. And in return, help me to treat others as favourably as You treat me, in Your Name I ask, thank You, Amen"

WHEN IT'S YOUR TIME FOR FAVOUR

God ignores protocol and defies logic

At this, she bowed down with her face to the ground. She asked him, "Why have I found such favour in your eyes that you notice me. foreigner?" Ruth 2:10

- 'I will look on you with favour and make you fruitful and increase your numbers, and I will keep my covenant with you. *Leviticus 26:9*
- May the favour of the Lord our God rest on us; establish the work of our hands for us, yes, establish the work of our hands. *Psalm 90:17*
- For He says, "In the time of my favour I heard you and in the day of salvation I helped you." I tell you, **now** is the time of God's favour, **now** is the day of salvation! *2 Corinthians 6:2*
- But He gives us more grace. That is why Scripture says: "God opposes the proud but shows favour to the humble." *James 4:6*
- When God approves of your life, even your enemies will end up shaking your hand (*favour*!) *Proverbs 16:7*

Time to Touch: Favour

It's been a long time coming but, dear reader, a change **is** sure to come and is definitely on its way! Sometimes for us to get the reaction we are seeking, there needs to be a primary action.

So this is the touch of faith you need to do:

- Stand up, lift your hands above your heads and just imagine there is a cloud of favour hovering right above you. For you to get it, you've got to reach!
- Stand on tip toe (but please, don't topple over!) and reach as high as you can.
- Stretch your arms, hands and fingers upwards, until you can almost touch it the favour cloud over your head.
- Grab as much as you can and pull it down towards you.
- Repeat this procedure, until you feel you have gathered enough favour you need to go forward
- Then step out in faith and GO FORWARD IN FAVOUR!

Now you have claimed favour, begin to think and speak it on a regular basis, until it begins to manifest from the realm of the Spirit, into your everyday life. Favour is the atmosphere you destined to live in.

God is lining things up for my favour!

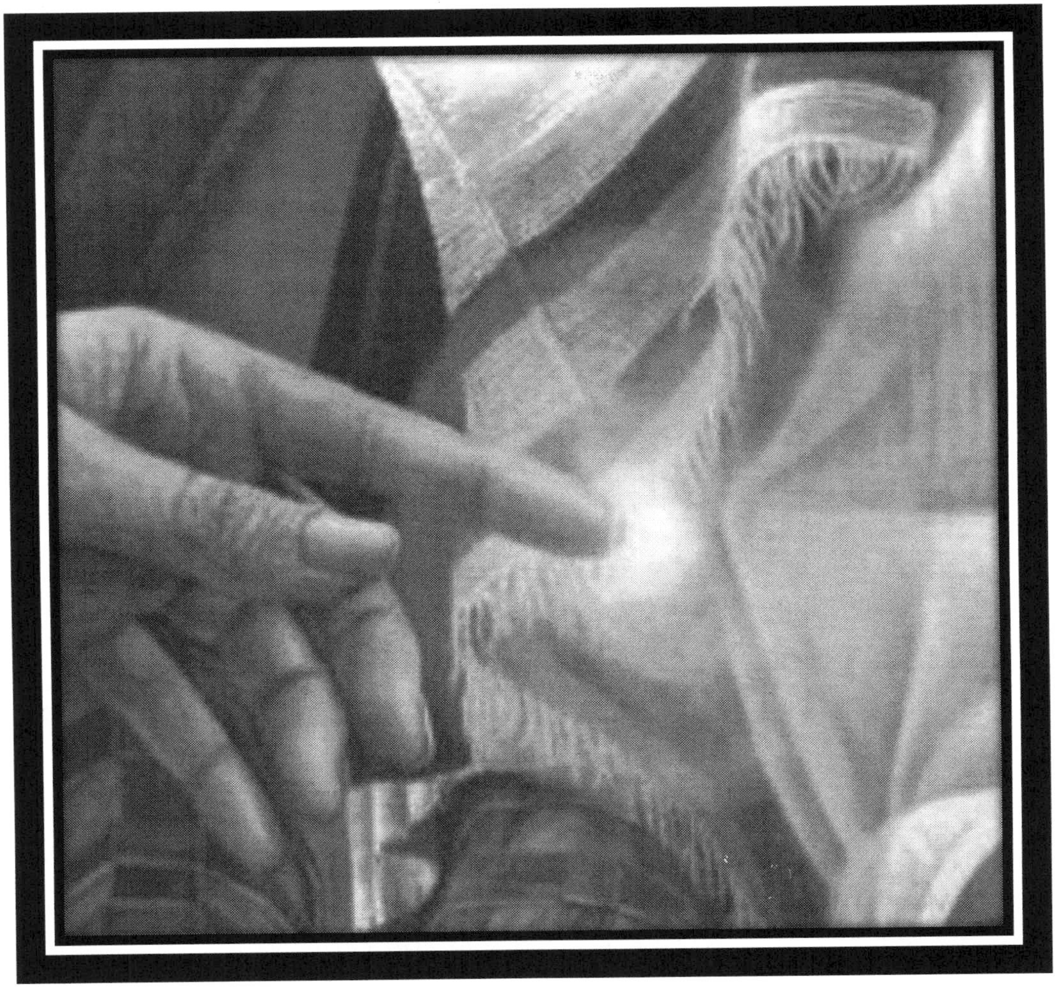

If a simple touch of faith can ignite favour in your life, then what are you waiting for?

3 Courage & Encouragement

Courage. Now that's a definitive word! It's one of those words which almost needs to be spoken in a deep, resonating bass voice. (Try saying it in a high pitch tone and you'll see what I mean!) **Courage** is defined as the quality of mind or spirit that enables a person to face difficulty, danger, pain, etc., without fear; it is the "stuff" from which the concept of "bravery" is made. Other words used for and in conjunction with this grand word include: *boldness, braveness, confidence, reckless, daring and strength of character*.

The word itself conjures up images of swashbuckling, dashing men who will take on a whole army, just to rescue a damsel in distress. Courage. Yes, we can all feel brave, bold, confident and even daring when the sun is shining, money is in our pockets, we're healthy, wealthy and wise and the world is our friend.

Ah, but should something or someone unexpected come our way, we suddenly find ourselves stumbling downwards from the dizzy heights of courage's' mountain top to end up, once more, having to feel our way through the slips, dips, thorns and hedges of life's dark valley moments. It is at such times, when the wind has been knocked out of us, when we feel that this is really the end – that we then need **encouragement**.

Definitions of this wonderful word include:

- To inspire with courage, spirit, or confidence: *His coach encouraged him throughout the marathon race to keep on running.*
- To stimulate by assistance, approval, etc.: *One of the chief duties of a teacher is to encourage students.*
- To promote, advance, or foster: *Poverty often encourages crime.*

You see, there will come a time when life has drained you dry of your courage; courage to stay in that job, that relationship, that marriage, that course, that ministry. There will come a time when your cup of courage will drain and empty and all you have left is a half-baked dream, an almost-completed goal and an "if only" vision. It is at those times we need en-couragement; an in-filling; a top up, a second draught of the sweet, heady nectar of courage, so we can be strengthened, empowered and emboldened to complete what we started.

In essence, when you help, or are helped, by giving or receiving words of encouragement, one key result is it leaves you or the person you being encouraged, noticeably bolder and braver. By giving (or receiving) **en**couragement, another level of courage is added to your own resources, so you are better equipped to stand firmer and go farther. If you feel in need of courage or would like a top up of **en**couragement, this section is just for you...

COURAGE SELDOM ROARS

While Encouragement keeps you moving

Take Courage, My Friend...

"Take courage my friend",
The wind whispered to me'
As I tried to shelter from life's storms
That were beating down on me...

"Take courage, my friend"
The stars sang from the sky
When the cold chill of fear
Echoed my heart's cry.

"Take courage, my friend",
The sun said to me,
As I toiled in the heat of the day
With no cloud to shelter or cover me

"Take courage, my friend"
I heard a whisper within my heart
When life had dealt another sharp blow
And my world fell apart.

It was then I realised courage was not outside
But was the inner reality of who I am!
All along I'd had the keys to release myself
From the pit of life, grief and shame!

Courage, like a trickle at first and then a mighty dam
Rushed out to water my own thirsty soul!
Like crystal clear water it came on and
Cleansed and made me whole!

If, like me, you're empty, worn and sad
And think you lack the courage to go on;
Reach deep down inside, into your heart mind
Believe courage will once again appear
Trust me when I tell you - it's not all gone!
"Take courage, my friend!"

Lisa Anthony-Rigsby

David was greatly distressed, for the men spoke of stoning him because the souls of them all were bitterly grieved, each man for his sons and daughters. But David encouraged and strengthened himself in the Lord his God. 1 Samuel 30:6

There are times when I feel sad, down and generally tired, but thankfully, a feeling is not a reality, is it? I therefore choose to be determined to ***rise*** above my feelings to recognize my God-given heritage as a child, a son/daughter of the King of Kings & Lord of Lords! It's at such times that we have to speak a positive change, based on the Word of God, into our own lives. God said (not me, God!), that "*...nothing can ever separate me from His love*" (**Romans 8:38**). What a delightful and wonderful promise! What a comfort to know that nothing I go through, have been through, or will ever go through, can ever separate from His love. Wow!

So I will take a leaf out of David's book and "encourage myself". It's so uplifting to know I have a God-given right and ability to comfort, encourage, , uphold, empower, hearten, cheer, support, promote, strengthen, fortify, reinforce, buttress and bolster myself, according to my needs and His goodness, love and grace! What a wonderful gift. Thank you Lord! This is a clarion call for action. Instead of feeling – and staying down – just ***dare*** to take courage and encourage yourself. You'll be glad you did.

"Father, I pray for courage as I begin this day, for I understand there is work to be done, burdens to be carried, feelings to be shared and joys to be celebrated. Grant me the courage to be silent that I may hear Your voice. To persevere, that I may share Your victory, and to remember, lest I forget, the way by which You have led me. And when this day is done, may I have the courage to see Your guiding hand in friendships made, hurts healed, and in the strength received and to be encouraged to keep on believing and trusting in You. Amen."

"Heavenly Father, many people see me as being bold, courageous, fearless and daring – but You alone know the truth! I lack the courage to be myself; I lack the courage to be honest with who I am. I pray for courage, Your courage, to do and be what You would have me to be, today and every day. Breathe Your courage into me that I may go further than my wildest dreams. I thank You for hearing me, I ask in Jesus' name, Amen"

"Help me to give a helping hand to lift someone along the way. Help me to walk with someone and to share their load. Let my words uplift and encourage fellow travellers with what they need, so they too can be encouraged in themselves. Father, we all need courage and encouragement. So flow through me and fill me, so I can fill others with the courage I receive from You. Thank You for hearing!"

STANDING WITH OTHERS IS EASY

It takes courage to stand alone

Be strong and of good courage, do not fear nor be afraid of them; for the LORD your God, He is the One who goes with you. He will not leave you nor forsake you." Deuteronomy 31:6

- Whether the land is rich or poor; and whether there are forests there or not, be of good courage. *Numbers 13:20*
- But the Israelites encouraged one another and again took up their positions where they had stationed themselves the first day. *Judges 20:22*
- You, LORD, hear the desire of the afflicted; You encourage them, and You listen to their cry, *Psalm 10:17*
- Wait on the LORD; be of good courage, and He shall strengthen your heart. Wait, I say, on the LORD! *Psalm 27:14*
- Be of good courage, and He shall strengthen your heart, all you who hope in the LORD. *Psalm 31:24*
- Everyone helped his neighbour and said to his brother, "Be of good courage!" *Isaiah 41:6*
- Finally, brothers and sisters, rejoice! Strive for full restoration, encourage one another, be of one mind, live in peace. And the God of love and peace will be with you. *2 Corinthians 13:11*
- Therefore encourage one another and build each other up, just as in fact you are doing. *1 Thessalonians 5:11*
- Your love has given me great joy and encouragement *Philemon 1:7*

Time to Touch: Courage & Encouragement

If you feel the fear, it's time to let it go! You can get some courage and be encouraged, right where you are, with these few simple steps

- ★ Right now, stand still... and stop. Stop what you are doing and stop carrying all the fears, worries, anxieties and stresses which have drained you of courage, and stopped you from being a blessing of encouragement to others
- ★ Take a deep, deep breath. As you do so, feel courage coming in and filling you from the crown of your head to the soul of your feet.
- ★ Hold the breath for a while and then, let it out, very, very slowly. Release all the negativity which is making you feel afraid and fearful.
- ★ Repeat the deep-breathing exercise a few more times and, when you are ready, affirm yourself with the following proclamation:

"I have the God-given ability to comfort, encourage, uplift, uphold, empower and hearten, cheer and support, promote and strengthen, fortify and reinforce myself, in Jesus name!"

Say it once, say it twice, then stand and it out loud, for the third time. What you are doing is a leap, a touch of faith, for it is time, YOUR time, to get courage and be encouraged!

Courage will only come
when faith takes the lead

4 Vision & Purpose

Any self-respecting personal development programme will have lots to say about the need to acquire these two essential elements of life – vision and purpose. Many people spend hundreds and even thousands of pounds in the search to know their vision and purpose. Yet, after we've "ticked the box" with regards to our respective career pathways and have spent years in a job we thought was our dream, we can still end up wondering ~ was this ever my vision? Have I really fulfilled my purpose? Or have I lost the ability to dream once more?

Vision is defined as "*the act or power of sensing with the eyes; the act or power of anticipating that which will or may come to be, e.g. as in a prophetic vision*". Vision takes us beyond our humdrum lives into realms of the impossible. The very word has the ability to take us back to our individual golden age of innocence. Here, we began to realise the world was made especially for us to walk onto its stage to do what it was we were created to do. We recall our dreams: vivid, imaginative, colourful conceptions and anticipations of visions of wealth, fame and glory. We were going to climb Everest! We were going to write *that* book, pen *that* song, design *that* outfit, create *that* car, build *that* house, take *that* holiday, on and on and on. Ah, vision! No need to look far to find it, for it's merely a glance, a breath, a prayer and a faith-touch away.

Vision then, deals with sight and, whilst many of us may have "20/20 vision" (with or without the aid of optical appliances), we recognise the cares of life have blinded us from going forward to reach our full potential. In the spring and summer of our lives, our internal vision is relatively focused and undimmed. Yet a marriage, children, mortgage, illness, the economy and some or all of life's seasonal issues keep us preoccupied and distracted from keeping our focus. It is then, in the transition from one season to another, as we dance from summer into autumn and slide towards the autumn and winter of our lives, we find our sight, our "vision" has somewhat dimmed. We become internally frustrated because the picture of who and what we wanted to be has become somewhat blurred and the picture begins to fade and lose focus.

So if, as you read this section, you realise you have somehow lost your sense of vision and misplaced your purpose, you're at the right place. If life has or is blinding you from reaching and achieving your dream, you're at the right page. If you look in the mirror and can't *see* the woman (or man!) you had imagined and hoped you'd be at the age you're now at, don't worry. It's not too late – it's time to dream dreams and revisit your vision.

Purpose is the other side of vision; it is our internal "get-up-and-go" mechanism so we can achieve our vision. Whereas vision may sit and "dream", purpose rolls up its sleeves, pulls on its trainers and says "hey, let's get going!" Definitions for the term purpose include:

- The reason for which something exists or is done, made, used, etc.
- An intended or desired result; end; aim; goal.
- Determination; resoluteness.
- The subject in hand; the point at issue.
- Practical result, effect, or advantage: to act to good purpose.

Sadly, because we often get caught up in the here and now, we forget the where and when we are supposed to be heading to. We've switched to "rear-view driving"; we're sitting at the wheel, but instead of looking ahead (vision and purpose), our eyes are locked onto the rear view mirror! By looking at what's behind, we've lost sight of our purpose, the direction we're meant to be heading in! But it's not too late to reconfigure and get a new boost of purpose! That's why vision and purpose work so well together! Synonyms for purpose include: *ambition, aspiration, design, desire, direction, intention, objective, plan, scheme, target* and a sense of *where one is heading.* It also implies: *strength of mind or will; a sense of decidedness, decisiveness, determination, doggedness, earnestness, firmness, fortitude, grit, iron will, obstinacy, perseverance, persistence, pluck, resoluteness, resolution, resolve, seriousness* and *will power.* In other words – once you make your mind, you **purpose** you are not going back!

Vision is where, what, how we want to be; **Purpose** is the map for us to get there!

Catch the Vision! Walk with Purpose! Picture this: You are finally getting married (your boyfriend has finally caught the vision). You begin to *envision*, to "see" yourself in *that* dress, you know, the one of your dreams. You imagine yourself gliding up the aisle to your beloved but you realise there's a little work to do in order to look the best you can in *that* dress! Purpose now begins to rev up vision's engine. You dust off your trainers, you get up a little earlier to tackle those extra inches which have crept up on you – in all the wrong places! Eating habits change, your mental thinking changes and your focus changes – why? You have now **caught** the ***vision*** and are now **walking** with ***purpose***! So, if you feel your vision is 1/20 and your purpose balloon has popped, then this chapter is definitely for you!

Catch the Vision! Walk with Purpose!

It's been so long since I have seen
The dreams, the longings, the depth of the real me!
It's been so long since I've walked with purpose, poise and direction
Towards the plans and ideas that were once my reality ...!

Caught up with catching up the latest this and that,
The in-thing that'll soon be the out-thing, the hottest craze and must-have fad.
But I'm walking blind, my vision almost gone;
As trying to survive just one more day, is no longer any fun.

Bills, emotions, careers – all have me running wild.
Yet, when I'm still, soul still, I can hear my inner child
Shouting down to me through the corridors of time:
"You can still catch the vision and walk in purpose! You've still got time!"

I laughed at first, as I saw my grey hairs, my broadening waist and my empty nest,
But the echo became more forceful and more robust!
"It's never too late to be still, so you can see;
So find your vision and live your life more purposefully"

And so that's why I'm here to share my story;
It's never too late to give up, take a chance, review, revise and see;
Because the meaning of life – YOUR life - is to catch your own vision,
To live your life with purpose, full and free!"
Lisa Anthony-Rigsby

ACTION!!!

If you recognise your need for a fresh vision and sense of purpose, God is more than willing to recalibrate your optical settings. Just as when you get new pair of glasses or contact lenses to correct your vision, what you thought was ordinary and blurred now begins to look brighter, more sharper, more defined. It's time, regardless your age, colour and creed, to focus and refocus! It's time to catch the vision and start to walk out the rest of your life with purpose!

"Lord, help me to see with divine 20/20 vision! To see beyond my here and now, beyond the why and when. Help me to know, recognise, see and understand exactly what my vision is, so I can begin to catch hold of ***the*** dream, goal, desire and ambition which fills my waking moments. Open my eyes – both spiritual and natural – to see and grasp opportunities as they come. Oh Father, may my vision be a mirror reflection of the plans, dreams and desires You have for me, Amen".

✞ "Like the blind man who cried after you when You walked this earth, I may not see, but oh, I have a vision! Like him, I desire what I've never known and have yet to experience – the opportunity to see! Please open my eyes and remove the scales. Make clear the dreams you have sown within me and may each fulfilment of each vision be a stepping stone into Your glorious will and purpose, Amen"

✞ "Just as a cup has a purpose, just as a pen has a purpose, just as a diamond has purpose, reveal what my purpose and plan is. Why am I here? Who am I meant to be? What is that I am meant to do? Father, as You remind me that my life has meaning and purpose, so let me do the same to those around me. Breathe new direction, purpose and vision into my very being. Give me strength to continue and not turn back. Give me wisdom to keep to walk the path set before me. Having caught the vision – Your vision - for a better and brighter future with You, grant me the grace to walk in it, with determination and purpose. In Your name I ask, Amen".

True purpose is realised when we can say...

"Write the vision and make it plain on tablets, that he may run who reads it. For the vision is yet for an appointed time; but at the end it will speak, and it will not lie. Though it tarries, wait for it; because it will surely come, it will not tarry" Habakkuk 2:2-3

- "And it shall come to pass afterward that I will pour out My Spirit on all flesh; your sons and your daughters shall prophesy, your old men shall dream dreams, your young men shall see visions. *Joel 2:28*
- The secret was revealed to Daniel in a night vision. So Daniel blessed the God of heaven. *Daniel 2:19*
- I make known the end from the beginning, from ancient times, what is still to come. I say, 'My purpose will stand, and I will do all that I please.' *Isaiah 46:10*
- So is my word that goes out from my mouth: it will not return to me empty, but will accomplish what I desire and achieve the purpose for which I sent it. *Isaiah 55:11*
- And we know that in all things God works for the good of those who love him, who have been called according to his purpose. *Romans 8:28*
- For it is God who works in you to will and to act in order to fulfil his good purpose. *Philippians 2:13*

Hold the Vision! Trust the Process!

LIVE LIFE WITH PURPOSE

Time to Touch: Vision & Purpose

It's time to take action, right where you are! Just as the woman pushed through the crowds to get her healing, so you are going to "push" through the crowds of your everyday life to get your vision so as to walk with purpose, for purpose and in purpose! (Now, read the following, then just do it!)

Close your eyes. There's a small table in front of you, which has two, bright and dazzling diamonds. One is engraved with a capital "**V**", the other with a capital "**P**", and they represent **vision** and **purpose** – YOUR vision and purpose. But as you reach out, your hand hits an invisible, micro thin sheet, preventing you from getting them. At this point, you can choose to sigh, shrug your shoulders and walk away... or you can stretch out your arms and hands as far as you can in front of you (lean forward, if you have too!), because you want, no, you need a touch from the Master for a renewed sense of vision and purpose.

That invisible micro thin sheet represents your own fears, insecurities, doubts and anxieties – all the negatives which life throws at you, to stop you knowing and becoming who you're meant to be. It's time to take drastic action:

- Sit and close your eyes
- Stretch, stretch... s.t.r.e.t.ch... your arms out in front of you, as far as you can.
- Extend your fingertips to touch them... that's it!
- Push your way and breakthrough whatever it is that is stopping you
- Grab the diamonds, one in each hand and them tightly in your hand. Make a fist and bring them to you. (Still keep your eyes closed; I know it's tempting to peep, but hold on a for a few seconds!)
- Place your fists on your lap, and then slowly, open your hands, one finger at a time.
- In your mind's eye, imagine the shimmer and glimmer of each brilliantly cut diamond in your hand – and smile!

Congratulations! You are now holding a new vision and a new purpose. Now open your eyes and prepare to walk towards your goal. It's what you were born to do....

5 Patience

Patience is a state of being we *choose* to be in, when facing times of distress, anxiety, worry, fear and all of life's negative foibles. We can choose to exercise patience from when we're waiting for a bus, a friend, a medical test, an exam result - and also when we have to deal with other people's "stuff". We need patience as we await the fulfilling of our dreams. We ought to take the patience path, when confronted with life's "fight or flight" situations. In those moments, patience is knowing that, in spite of life's manure, we will come up "smelling of roses!"

Some characterisations regarding the term ***patience***, or to ***be patient***, include:

1. The quality of being patient, as the bearing of provocation, annoyance, misfortune, or pain, without complaint, loss of temper, irritation, or the like.
2. An ability or willingness to suppress restlessness or annoyance when confronted with delay: *to have patience with a slow learner.*
3. Quiet, steady perseverance; even-tempered care; diligence: *to work with patience.*

Patience is, choosing to deliberately and willingly ignore and put aside our natural and instinctive responses to life's irritations, to walk the road less travelled. A modern definition of patience is "*stickability*", which is the ability to endure something or persevere in something. So, what are some of the situations and circumstances which are currently trying your patience? What is it that has you on edge, that has you practically holding on by your fingernails? Indeed, what is that is helping you to hold on – and, more importantly, what is holding you? If this describes where you are, you really need patience! It is one of life's guard rails, to help you stay within your lane and on the path, so you do not fall off, out or over the edge.

So if you are holding onto the last, frayed thread of your patience. If you find your patience is wearing so thin, you can practically see through it. If you want to throw in the towel and just call it a day - please, dear reader, wait a few more moments. This section is for YOU...

Waiting on You Lord

I seek your face Father and I wait upon you,
For those who wait on you will renew their strength.
Thank You Father that you are my Provider.
There is not a need I have that you do not know of.
For your thoughts are ever towards me and your banner of love cover me.
Thank You Father, for your word assures me "Let none that wait on
You be ashamed." My heart waits for you.
Lord disappointment is impossible with you.
You are good unto them that waits for you.
Therefore I will look to the Lord, I will wait for God of my Salvation.
My Soul waits thou only upon God!
In the loving name of Jesus I pray, Amen.

Nathalie Byer

PATIENCE IS BITTER

But the fruit is always sweet

… Patience Proverbs …

Patience is the greatest of all virtues.
Cato the Elder (234 BC - 149 BC)

Patience is the companion of wisdom.
Saint Augustine (354 AD - 430 AD)

Though patience be a tired mare, yet she will plod.
William Shakespeare (1564 - 1616), Henry V, Act II, sc. 1

Have patience with all things, but, first of all with yourself.
Saint Francis de Sales, 1567-1622

Your eyes are bulging, your breathing is fast and shallow. Sweat is pouring and your adrenaline pumping. You are... at... the... end... of... your... last... nerve! Every limb is trembling, and you can feel the rope burn, as it slides painfully from your grasp. **STOP**! Before you let go, drop off, roll over or give in to your natural fight or flight tendencies, why not turn the situation around and take time for an urgent prayer break? God has heard your cry for patience and is right by your side, waiting to walk you through.

LIFE'S GREATEST BLESSINGS
Are always seasoned with Patience

"Father! I know I'm about to lose it, big time! Help me to hold on just a little bit longer! Help me to keep my cool in the midst of the heat of this moment/situation/circumstance! Help me hold it together, especially the last nerve that is tried and frayed! Help me to keep my focus on You, Your Word and Your love, so I can get through this. Just when I think it's all over and I can come up for air, something/someone seems to pull me back. Father, I cannot do this in my own strength, so I come to You, in need of Your brand of patience and endurance. Help me to pass this test – please! Amen!"

✞ I'm waiting for the storm to pass and I feel I've been here forever! I'm trying to wait with a smile but it's hard. I'm trying to wait with hope, but it's hard. I'm trying to wait with love but oh God, it's really hard. When everything seems to fail me, when everything seems to want to back up and back off, when my dreams, hopes, desires and wishes have all dissolved like morning mist in the early morning sun... I choose to look up, I choose to dry my eyes, straighten my back and retain my position to wait patiently, in You and on You, for You to come through, Amen!

✞ Right now, I can't see past the anger, hurt and rage I am feeling! I want to do something, right here and now and I'm close, so very close, to losing my patience, temper, my cool – everything! So my prayer ain't pretty but it's honest and from my heart – HELP!

For whatever things were written before were written for our learning, that we through the patience and comfort of the Scriptures might have hope. Now may the God of patience and comfort grant you to be like-minded toward one another, according to Christ Jesus. *Romans 15:4-6*

- 🕮 Now may the Lord direct your hearts into the love of God and into the patience of Christ. *2 Thessalonians 3:5*
- 🕮 My brethren, count it all joy when you fall into various trials, knowing that the testing of your faith produces patience. But let patience have its perfect work, that you may be perfect and complete, lacking nothing. *James 1:2-4*
- 🕮 A person's wisdom yields patience; it is to one's glory to overlook an offense. *Proverbs 19:11*
- 🕮 The end of a matter is better than its beginning, and patience is better than pride. *Ecclesiastes 7:8*

Time to Touch: Patience

Everything in you is ready for "flight or fight"! The situation is volatile, you're almost at the end of your rope and feel you're about to explode! Stop! There is another option: PATIENCE. You can ***choose*** to ride out the storm. You can ***choose*** to wait it out. You can ***choose*** to practice patience. It's at these times, where you learn to allow the pain and perplexity of your heart to reach out and touch the hem of His garment.

- ✯ Imagine you are in a circle and outside are all the things that are seeking to draw you out by making you lose your patience.
- ✯ But before you act or react – remember, you have a choice: to answer them and lose – or to stay with the circle of God's love and let patience win the day.... It's your call.
- ✯ In the centre of the circle is a nice, comfy armchair with your name on it and an ice-chilled drink and a few nibbles on a side table, just for you. Now, you can either get up in rage and anger to "address the issues" ... or sit and be still, calm, cool and collected in your armchair, in the patience zone of life. It's your call.

Use this word picture whenever you feel you are about to lose your cool. Choose to stay balanced, grounded and focused in the centre of God's love. Use and allow the gift of God's patience to keep you grounded in the midst of life's storms, situations and circumstances.

6 Faith

Now this is a big topic, one where theologians and church folks wet their lips as they start to expound, while "ordinary folks" like you and me, sit silently, waiting for them to give an answer we can understand. Many of us have heard that faith is the *"...substance of things hoped for, the evidence of things unseen*" (Hebrews 11:1). Well. now that we have the answer to what faith is, we can move onto another section - or can we? For although that **is** the answer, based on the Word of God, how many of us can truly say that we have "evidence" or "substance"?

So let me ask you again... what exactly ***is*** faith? Most definitions of faith includes such terms as "*confidence or trust*" in a person, thing and/or idea and concept. Interestingly, it is even defined as *"...belief that is not based on proof*", which seems to contradict our opening premise. So, which is it?

Before you answer, consider this: when you get on the bus or train, you assume it will take you to where you are going; that's ***faith***. When you enter a room and sit on a chair, you automatically believe it will hold you up – that's ***faith***! By ***faith***, we enter a huge metal contraption and travel thousands of miles, either in the air or on the sea, believing we will get to our destination safely. Oh yes, we overeat at Christmas and New Year and still expect to get into our "little black dresses" by mid-January; trust me, that's ***faith***! You see we are, by the very nature of our humanness, creatures of faith! It was ***faith*** which was the catalyst and the launch pad for the many inventions we now enjoy today. It was ***faith*** in an unspoken hope and desire for something better and beyond ourselves, which ignited social change in many cultures and societies.

From a personal perspective, ***faith*** propels a single parent with young children to go back to school, in order to gain a better education and benefit their family in the long run. It is ***faith*** which gives you the energy to keep on dreaming your impossible dream. Faith sees beyond the here and now to what can be. It's the faint glimmer of light, of hope, flickering in the midst of dark times. It is an inner peace of mind which keeps us from going adrift on the sea of life. Faith is the Mona Lisa smile in the midst of mayhem, misery, doubt and worry.

Ahhh, what a precious gift faith is! We are all born with it but life has numerous ways to chip at it, knock it down and to squeeze it out of us. But it doesn't have to be that way for you – or me. All we need is simply the DESIRE to want to have it ~ and He will do the rest.

Walk of Faith

Your love O Lord reaches to the heavens.
Your faithfulness reaches to the skies glory!
I will speak of Your faithfulness and salvation.
I will sing of Your great love forever.

You are mighty O Lord and Your faithfulness surrounds me.
To proclaim Your love in the morning and Your faithfulness at night is the desire of my heart.
I praise You, for You are the One who makes my faith to grow.
I ask You Lord, to help me stay in Your Word so my faith can grow.

I declare the entrance of Your Word into my life
That it produces growth and maturity.
I confess that if I live by faith and not by sight,
I daily confess what the Word of God
Says and believe it shall come to pass.

Lord, I ask that you will help me to hold on
To my confession of faith and to remember,
Faith comes from hearing the message.
Thank You Lord, for all things are possible through you.

Nathalie Byer

This is it. You're in a place where your strength has gone, your patience has run out and you feel you have nothing left with which to fight with. What now? Faith has died – or has it? If you are silent and soul, body, emotions and spirit still, you will hear, from deep within, a still, small voice.

Just open up and let It in. It's the voice of faith. Don't shut it out or shut it up! Faith is your internal life coach, your personal mentor, your intuitive counsellor. And it's sent to help you believe and get back in the game!

FEED YOUR FAITH

And starve your fears!

"Father, I believe – help my unbelief! I can't see it but I have to believe it; I can't touch it, but I can feel it; I can't taste it but I can digest it. It is the substance of my faith, it is the evidence of all my hopes, dreams and desires. Father, increase my faith beyond my wildest dreams. Thank You. Amen!"

Father, help me to understand the wonderful gift of faith You have given to me. Help me to recognise and to utilise it in every area of my life. Let my words match up with the faith I have, so I speak, not based on what or where I may be, but on the reality of what I want to see in my life. Help me to realise that faith is more than a positive mental attitude. It is an essential and intrinsic part of my very being. As You spoke things into being, help me to realise that, with and by Your help, I can do the same in faith. This I ask in Your Name, Amen"

Now if God so clothes the grass of the field, which today is, and tomorrow is thrown into the oven, will He not much more clothe you, O you of little faith? ***Matthew 6:30***

- But Jesus turned around, and when He saw her He said, "Be of good cheer, daughter; your faith has made you well." And the woman was made well from that hour. *Matthew 9:22*
- Then He touched their eyes, saying, "According to your faith let it be to you." *Matthew 9:29*
- So Jesus said to them, "… I say to you, if you have faith as a mustard seed, you will say to this mountain, 'Move from here to there,' and it will move; and nothing will be impossible for you. *Matthew 17:20*
- So Jesus answered and said to them, "Assuredly, I say to you, if you have faith and do not doubt, you will not only do what was done to the fig tree, but also if you say to this mountain, 'Be removed and be cast into the sea,' it will be done. *Matthew 21:21*
- And the apostles said to the Lord, "Increase our faith." … So Jesus answered and said to them, "Have faith in God *Luke 17:5 and Mark 11:22*
- But I have prayed for you, that your faith should not fail…" *Luke 22:32*
- So then faith comes by hearing, and hearing by the word of God. *Romans 10:17*
- (May) your faith … not be in the wisdom of men but in the power of God. *1 Corinthians 2:5*
- Watch, stand fast in the faith, be brave, be strong. *1 Corinthians 16:13*
- For by grace you have been saved through faith, and that not of yourselves; it is the gift of God, *Ephesians 2:8*
- Above all, taking the shield of faith with which you will be able to quench all the fiery darts of the wicked one. *Ephesians 6:16*
- If we are faithless, He remains faithful; He cannot deny Himself. *2 Timothy 2:13*

FOR WE WALK BY FAITH

And not by hearing, sound or sight

Time to Touch: Faith

It seems so long since you believed, I mean, really believed. Back then, it was a way of life. As a child, you had faith your parents would feed you. You had faith that day would always follow night and winter would (eventually!) turn into spring. You even had faith when you first said yes – but sadly, your life experiences have caused you to doubt.

But wait. There is within you, an awareness, a slight stirring, a small voice, a faint hope, a tiny glimmer of light. It's strange, yet somehow familiar, like a face you recognise but can't remember from where. That familiar feeling, is faith. It's is God's gift, seeking to come back home. It wants to finish its mission and take you to newer heights and brighter dimensions. Reaching out to faith is not hard at all, especially if it's reaching out to you.

- ✯ Where you are sitting right now, just put your hands on your stomach and breathe in. Feel your hands move outwards as life-giving air fills your body.
- ✯ Now breathe out and hold your hands in against your stomach as you do so. As you exhale, gently push out as much air as you can. The air leaving you represents all your inner doubts, worry, fears and anxieties from the very belly of your being.
- ✯ Now take the deepest breath you can and fill yourself with faith! (It might be hard to begin with, especially if you have not been faith-breathing as you should have been),
- ✯ Don't give up, but take another deep breath, and another, and another. As you do so, let each fresh breath of faith refill and inflate every dream, hope, desire, and ambition lying dormant within you.

Today is your faith-filling day! Touch the hem of His garment! Breathe and be filled, in Jesus' name!

Faith is always the first step ....
Even when you don't see the staircase

7 Times & Seasons

This section is for those of us who may be at a crossroad in our lives, which could include:

- A new job;
- Redundancy or retirement;
- A new friendship, relationship or marriage;
- A leaving, separation or divorce;
- A new birth or another (maybe unexpected) arrival
- The sudden or expected loss of a loved one.

Whatever you may be facing – or have faced – this section is for you. It is all about timing, *your* timing, and as you reach out to "Touch the Hem of His Garment", may you be encouraged to go through to your next level...your next season.

So what time is it?

Ancient Greece had two words for time: **Chronos** and **Kairos**. ***Chronos*** refers to chronological or sequential time, whilst ***Kairos*** was used to define opportunity, a moment of indeterminate time in which something special is anticipated and/or happens. **Chronos** is *quantitative*, as reading this book may take a couple of hours, whereas **Kairos** focuses on the *qualitative* nature of time, in that, reading this book is just what you need and has definitely come at the right time for you (pardon the pun!)

But timing is crucial if you want to achieve and press forward to be who and what you were designed and created to be. You worked and studied for a specific vocation – but "life" happened. You married/had a child/relocated/needed to pay off your school fees/just wanted to get money, etc. The reasons were probably legitimate then, but now, you're beginning to realise you've outgrown the time and season you are currently in – just like those jeans you've got stashed at the bottom of the drawer! Seasons change – but it's all good! As winter melts into spring, so the sunny, heady and carefree days of summer shimmer and change into the sublime beauty and wealth of autumn. Time and seasons are what life is all about.

In Greek mythology, Kairos was depicted as a young man with small wings on his shoulders, a long lock of hair over his face, but no hair on the top or back of his head. So when you saw Kairos coming, it was an **opportunity** to grab him by the hair as he flew by, because, once he'd passed, you would not be able to grab him, as he had no hair to grab or hold onto! This is the genesis of the old saying, "How time flies". Kairos would fly in - but there was no guarantee you would be able to hold or keep him, because when he had gone, he was permanently gone. What a striking, yet disturbing image. For whether we realise it or not, wasted Kairos moments are wasted opportunities to grow. For once the moment has gone, it's gone!

This section will help you recognise the opportunities stored up in the times and seasons of your life. It will help you appreciate, recognise and prepare for opportunities of expectancy, possibility and from a spiritual perspective, God's activity. Kairos time is when we begin to sense God is desperately seeking to get our attention so that we can progress to the next phase. So, if you've been feeling that "something's in the air", don't ignore the feeling; just push through your current situation and circumstance, to walk into what God has for you.

GOD'S CLOCK IS NOT LIKE OURS

Never a day late, He's always on time!

Seasons in Life

To everything in life there is a season
With every phase a purpose and reason
When one season ends a new one will begin
Gaining wisdom from where we have been

A season to press forward to what lies ahead
Leaving the past behind and by Jesus being led
A season to labour in the harvest field
And a time to rest while in comes the yield

A season to weep and a time to rejoice
A time to be silent and a time to lift up our voice
A season to meditate on God's love and His word
A time to tell the gospel to others as you have heard

A season to be healthy, robust, and strong
A time of weariness and pain and for Heaven long
A season to abound and a time to suffer need
All the while ploughing to sow the gospel seed

A season to be active and a time to be still
All things according to God's perfect time and will
A season to be born and a time to die
When we fly away and go to our home on high

Nathalie Byer

EMBRACE THE SEASON

You are currently living in!

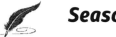

Riiiiiiinnnnngggg! Hey you, yes you, YOU! Life's alarm clock is going off. It's action time. No, don't hit the snooze button – again. It is time to get up, wipe the sleep from your eyes and get with the programme, YOUR programme! You have slept long enough, dreaming your dreams, goals and opportunities away. Every time you made an effort to move forward, you just let it slip through your fingers. Well, no more. You do not know if time and chance will come again. *Carpe diem* - seize the day! GET UP! This is the time and season, ***your*** time and season, for action. Get up, get up, get up – Kairos is coming - do not let it pass you by.

"I've wasted so much time in procrastination and lying to myself, saying I'll do this and that, only to let myself down. God, in the midst of all of this, You have kept me going, because You know my potential. Sorry for letting so many opportunities, chances, breaks and openings slip through my fingers but today, I'm asking for yet another chance, one more chance. Please don't give up on me. Help me to make it, to complete the dream and to be successful, within the assigned times and allotted seasons. Thank You and Amen."

✞ "Father of all time and eternity, I come. I feel that a change is about to happen: it's in the very air I breath, I'm hearing snippets in conversations and even in songs! But I need Your help to recognise when to move, because to move too soon or too late, may cause me to miss the opportune time to act. So I ask you to guide and direct me. Prompt me and let me know without a shadow of a doubt when, where and how, is the right time to move. And Father, please remove all fear and doubt. Help to hear the alarm in my internal clock so I can be up and ready for my Kairos time and season, Amen!"

[*Everything Has Its Time*] To everything there is a season, a time for every purpose under heaven. *Ecclesiastes 3:1*

- For I know the thoughts that I think toward you, says the Lord, thoughts of peace and not of evil, to give you a future and a hope. *Jeremiah 29:11*
- He changes times and seasons; he deposes kings and raises up others. He gives wisdom to the wise and knowledge to the discerning. *Daniel 2:21*
- I returned and saw under the sun that the race is not to the swift, nor the battle to the strong, nor bread to the wise, nor riches to men of understanding, nor favour to men of skill; but time and chance happen to them all. *Ecclesiastes 9:11*
- Therefore, as we have opportunity, let us do good to all, especially to those who are of the household of faith. *Galatians 6:10*
- Be very careful, then, how you live—not as unwise but as wise, making the most of every opportunity, because the days are evil. Therefore do not be foolish, but understand what the Lord's will is. *Ephesians 5:15-17*

Time to Touch: Times & Seasons

It's as simple as looking at the watch on your wrist. You have to realise that time is going; both Chronos and Kairos are passing, and the timely question is: what are **YOU** doing about it?

Touching the hem of His garment is an indication, your indication, of your newfound determination to make each second, each minute, each hour, day, week, month and each year, count. Why? Because contained in each capsule of Chronos time, **your** change, **your** opportunity and **your** Kairos moment is waiting for you, to reach out, grab it and run with it.

So, whenever anyone asks you what time is it, simply smile and say, "It's Kairos time!"

The bad news is ~ time flies!
The good news is ~ God is the pilot!

8 Victory

Ah, the sweet taste of victory is something we aspire to and long for. It's the dreamed of, and hoped for, result of the long, hard struggle we are currently been embroiled in. It is the utopia of whatever we have been seeking to achieve.

Victory is opening an envelope to find you have passed your exams, your application has been successful and you got the job! It's the email which says your book has (finally!) been accepted! It's the needle on the scale which confirms you have finally lost those last 10lbs and are now at your desired weight! It's the phone call to say, the test is positive and the baby is on the way. It is also that simple moment of clarity when you have just accomplished the ironing / mowing / washing up - and can now take a well-deserved break! Ahhh, now *that's* the sweet taste of victory!

So you get the picture, right? Victory is the fulfilment of what you have been working, sweating and striving towards, over long days and lonesome nights, weeks, months and years. No, it was not easy; but, as you stand on the podium to receive your well-deserved reward, you no longer remember the pains and aches, the sweat and tears, the mid-night cries and the mid-day droughts. No, you realise it was all part of the process, *your* process, for you to get to where you now are. Victory!

General definitions for victory include a "*final and complete superiority in a war or military engagement*" as well as "*success attained in a contest or struggle or over an opponent, obstacle, or problem*". Wow! That is ***you***, right there! Look back over your life and you will see how far you have come, through many dangers, toils and snares, nonetheless – victory - you are here! You may have a few battle scars and a limp or two, but you are here! For many others, who started out with you, fell away and are no longer in the race, Yet you, thank God, are here. You, thank God, have made it this far.

To help you appreciate your victory, I share the following synonyms, to once again remind you that you are a miracle, and should not take your victory for granted:

Victory, conquest, triumph – all refer to a successful outcome of a current and/or ongoing struggle.

- **Victory** suggests the decisive defeat of an opponent in a contest of any kind: *victory in battle; a football victory.*
- **Conquest** implies the taking over of control by the victor, and the obedience of the conquered: *a war of conquest; the conquest of Peru.*
- **Triumph** implies a particularly outstanding victory: *the triumph of a righteous cause; the triumph of justice.*

Nothing illustrates this more, than the ancient Greek and Roman games. Here, athletes competed for the ultimate prize which was not a gold, silver or even a bronze medal, but the only prize – a laurel wreath, which was the victor's crown. Although made of twigs and leaves, being awarded the laurel crown was the ultimate prize. It was the main reason why these ancient athletes strained every muscle and sinew in their body to transform their lifestyle and physique, in order to attain it. They underwent rigorous training, a stoic diet and a punishing regime – but for them, it was worth it all. They are matched by today's modern athletes who compete in for national, world, Commonwealth and Olympic glory. For some, just being picked to represent their national team is victory enough, much less winning a bronze, silver or the coveted gold medal. It's all about competing to *win*. It's all about competing for the *prize*! Victory!

They forgo evenings out and socialising - they have a goal and are training to *win*. They watch their diet and up their training programme - because they are on a mission and their number one goal is to *win*. Many give up their full time jobs and have to offload their responsibilities onto long-suffering partners – because they *know* it will be worth it all in the end – when they *win*. Ah, the sweet, sweet allure of Victory!

You too have had to give up, put aside and leave behind some things – and people - in order to win. You have had to make some major adjustments to get your personal "laurel" crown of victory. It was not easy; but long, hard and lonely. But, congratulations! Well done! You have triumphed! You've conquered. Victory, at last, is yours!

The March of Victory

We were bought for a price
The blood of Jesus Christ
Who gave His life for you and me
He who died on Calvary

That second day in MOR
God's presence was just as strong
The choir were leading the worship songs
People were jumping and clapping
Giving God the highest praise
Everyone was happy that God was back

The psalmist brought people to their feet
As the march was of Victory
The battlefield that we marched on
God had already won
Together united as one
Claiming the victory

The Glory of the Lord was proclaimed
And we could have it
If we prayed for it in Jesus name
How great is our God
Just have faith and believe and you will see
Maxine Yearwood-Bailey

THE HARDER THE BATTLE
The sweeter the victory

Victory is in the air, you can practically taste it! It is the culmination of all the sweat, blood and tears you have had to expend, to get here. But, hold on, wait a minute! There is a slight hitch, a little hold-up. It is usually the *last* mile, the *last* push, the *last* few pounds, which is the hardest part of the journey. Ladies and gentlemen, it is at this juncture, when we are soooo close to victory, that we tend to give up and regress, often ending up further back than where we first started. But, do not despair: that was then - this is now! Right now, it is time for serious action. It is time for you to get back up and to get back in the game! You have been inactive for too long now. Your time out is officially over. Your next stop, is **VICTORY**!

"Father, it's been so long, so hard, so traumatic! I can see the finishing line, I can almost hear the cheers of the crowd who have supported me along each lap of my journey. But, oh Father, I am so very tired of having gone this long, this far and this continuous, and I really don't think I can make it to the end. I'm just so tired. And, it's in this weariness of spirit, tiredness of mind and fatigue of body, I simply ask You to be the wind beneath my wings. Give the final push, give me the necessary drive. Please be my second wind to make it through. I *know* I can, I *know* I must, make it. Thank you, Father, Amen"

✞ "Woooowie, we did it, Father, we did it! I just gotta thank you for bringing me this far! As I hold the trophy in my trembling hands, suddenly ***all*** the pain, the labour, the struggles, the mishaps, the misunderstandings, the sleepless nights and weary days, are only a small price to have paid for the victory – ***our*** victory - cos I know I could ***not*** have finished, without You by my side. Thank You for giving me the winning edge and the victor's determination to make it. I know that with You by my side, I have many other victories to win, and a victor's crown to enjoy! Just give me grace, Your grace, to make it across the finishing line. Help me Father, help me to make it, Amen"

Blessed is the man who endures temptation; for when he has been approved, he will receive the crown of life which the Lord has promised to those who love Him. *James 1:11-13*

- But thanks be to God, who gives us the victory through our Lord Jesus Christ. *1 Corinthians 15:57*
- Yours, O LORD, is the greatness, the power and the glory, the victory and the majesty; for all that is in heaven and in earth is Yours; Yours is the kingdom, O LORD, and You are exalted as head over all. *1 Chronicles 29:11*
- And also if anyone competes in athletics, he is not crowned unless he competes according to the rules. *2 Timothy 2:5*
- For whatever is born of God overcomes the world. And this is the victory that has overcome the world ~ our faith. *1 John 5:4*

The first and best victory is to conquer **self**

Plato

Time to Touch: Victory

You've made it this far... but you know the race isn't over yet. As you stretch your aching muscles and massage your throbbing head at the thought of yet another punishing mile, another push up, another bench press (whether real or literal), I want to you to pause long enough to touch the hem of His garment.

- Put your hands in a prayer position and as your palms touch, press them together
- Imagine you're pressing against the struggle, stress and strain that is ahead of you, those things which you need to overcome in order to succeed.
- Now, keeping the heels of your palms together, open your hands apart, to let your hands form a large "V".
- As you do so, imagine yourself opening up to *every* victory you have prayed and longed for!

It's that simple. All you need do, is touch His hem with your desire to win and start to run the race before you. Baby, you are already programmed to win! Ready... steady...GO! Victory is guaranteed!

When you get to the top,
you've only just begun! **Victory!**

9 Truth

Most of us who like to watch TV court-based dramas are familiar with the phrase "...to tell the truth, the whole truth and nothing but the truth". However, as the plot unfolds, we find the main characters speaking anything, but the truth!

So, what exactly IS truth? Definitions for truth include:

1. The true or actual state of a matter: *He tried to find out the truth.*
2. Conformity with fact or reality; verity: *the truth of a statement.*
3. A verified or indisputable fact, proposition, principle, or the like: *mathematical truths.*
4. The state or character of being true.
5. Actuality or actual existence.

It is what it is. It is seeing and saying the same thing. An old West Indian proverb states: "Don't give me a 6 for a 9". In other words, do not tell me it ***is***, when you know it's ***not***. Truth, absolute truth, is the essence of life and the only measure which truly defines us. And interestingly enough, even though we may struggle to live a life of truth, we can usually perceive the absence of it, in any given situation.

Case in point: You are running late for work and decide to tell a "white lie", you say the trains were delayed, when you conveniently forgot you were hitting the snooze button for over an hour. By making the conscientious decision to tell a "white lie" - and by the way, lying is *not* something that is colour-coded, as a lie is a lie is a lie - you have decided to lie first and foremost to yourself and so you set the benchmark by which life will mark you.

Your body reacts to lies, simply because we are programmed to tell the truth. So when you tell your boss that your train/bus/bicycle or whatever was "delayed", "you" might lie, but your body's autonomic nervous system simply cannot! And so, as the untruth hangs in the air, your body is in a traumatic state, as it undergoes certain physiological responses in its attempt to deceive. You avoid eye contact, your breathing gets shallow and your sweat glands goes into overdrive – all because you lied. Would it not have been easier to have told the truth? Remember, truth, like confession, is "good for the soul but maybe bad for the reputation!

When God chose to reveal Himself to Moses, He defined Himself as *"...the LORD, the LORD God, merciful and gracious, longsuffering, and abounding in goodness and truth"* (*Exodus 34:6*). Being made in His image, means He has programmed key elements into us. Truth, which is the quintessential essence of who He is, is therefore a vital element within the very fibre of mankind.

So, it's time to "fess up and get real. The truth is, God wants us to be like Him, to live like Him, to love like Him – and to be truthful, like Him. If you have not been truthful with others, including and especially yourself, now is time to change your talk and your walk.

TRUTH COSTS NOTHING
But a lie costs everything

Truth is...

If you touch me with words that lie
And eyes that cannot quite connect
I will know you are not quite what you say are
And that truth, is something, you've never met.

If you hold me with unclean hands
And walk beside me with wavering feet
I will know you are not quite where you'd hoped to land
And that your journey is still incomplete.

If your heart beats irregularly when lying still,
As the grains of time slowly fall
I pray you'll have time to hear and respond to
Truth's faint voice when to you it finally calls....
Lisa Anthony-Rigsby

You have hidden behind a facade for so long, you barely know who you are! You have built walls with bricks fashioned from your white lies and half-truths, in order to protect yourself. It worked – for a while. It was fun – for a while. But today, yes, *this* day, is your chance to come out from behind whatever mask you have been wearing. Today, yes, this day, is your chance to begin to embrace the truth of *who*, *what* and *where* you are. Isn't it funny, but what you have been avoiding, could well be the one thing you so desperately need - TRUTH!

Father, I've lived a lie for so long, it almost seems like the truth! I've believed the lies I'd been told from when I was a child; the lies I was told at school that I'd never amount to much; the lies I read about in the papers; the lies I hear in the media; the lies I've carried from my last relationship that no one would ever want me, need me ~ or love me. Oh Father of truth, I come to you for help to leave the lies behind, so I can walk in the light of truth…Your truth. Hear the honesty of my heart. Thank You"

- Father God, why does it hurt so much to tell the truth? Why do lies come so easily to me? I say I love the truth but honestly, it's the lie which springs so easily to my lips. From today, I sincerely ask for your help, to recognise and to live by, that rare, precious jewel – truth. It won't be easy but Father, I cannot and do not want to live this lie any more. Help me to live the reality of your truth in my life. Amen.

- I'm scared to tell the truth. I am scared to expose my inner most feelings, thoughts – the real me. I am scared of being vulnerable and open and honest and … real. I struggle to be honest with You, Father God, and yet, I am still drawn, by Your heart of love and truth, to come, just as I am, and to open my heart to You. So, it's from the midst of my untruthfulness, that I humbly ask You to hear my faint whisper of truth, when I say I need You, in every area of my life. Thank You for being a God of truth, love and mercy to me. Amen.

But the hour is coming, and now is, when the true worshipers will worship the Father in spirit and truth; for the Father is seeking such to worship Him. God is Spirit, and those who worship Him must worship in spirit and truth." *John 4:23-24*

- He is the Rock, His work is perfect; for all His ways are justice, a God of truth and without injustice; righteous and upright is He. *Deuteronomy 32:4*
- Lead me in Your truth and teach me, for You are the God of my salvation; on You I wait all the day. *Psalm 25:5*
- These are the things you shall do: Speak each man the truth to his neighbour; Give judgment in your gates for truth, justice, and peace. *Zechariah 8:16*
- And you shall know the truth, and the truth shall make you free." *John 8:32*
- Jesus said to him, "I am the way, the truth, and the life. No one comes to the Father except through Me. *John 14:6*
- If we say that we have fellowship with Him, and walk in darkness, we lie and do not practice the truth....if we say that we have no sin, we deceive ourselves, and the truth is not in us. *1 John 1:6, 8*
- I have no greater joy than to hear that my children walk in truth. *3 John 1:4*

HURT ME WITH THE TRUTH

Rather than comfort me with a lie

Time to Touch: Truth

It's time to face the truth, your truth…God's truth of who you really are. (*Read the following first, then do them as a point of contact*):

- ✯ Close your eyes and cover your face with your hands. The darkness you see represents the lies that have been told to you, the lies you've told yourself, the lies you have been living. Not one ray of truth to lighten your way – but thank God, all is not lost!

- ✯ With your hands covering your face, open your eyes. Rays of light, rays of truth now appear through the prison bars of your fingers.

- ✯ Finally, remove your hands and enjoy the light! Look around you! It's light! It's truth! Just reach out to the One Who is the essence of truth itself and let Him guide you into all truth.

It's time to touch the hem of His garment and let the His Truth cover you…

IF YOU WANT ME TO LIE FOR YOU

Do not be surprised when I lie to you

Take time to search and find the ...

For the truth will set you free...

10 Brokenness, Grief & Loss

No dictionary, general definition or interpretation is needed here. The death of a loved one, a relationship, a job – whatever is important to you – can leave you broken, grief-stricken and with an overwhelming sense of loss. Whilst all of us may respond differently to the same stimuli, in this case grief and loss, there is a shared sense of emptiness, longing, sadness even confusion at what has happened.

There are a number of unanswered questions, a constant replaying of images, situations and scenarios in your mind of the "*woulda, coulda, shoulda*" variety. A sense of betrayal, bitterness and even anger – towards the person, yourself and even God, who you feel could, should and *ought* to have stepped in to stop the loss.

You're tired of hearing common place platitudes and well-meaning but stale sentiments. You are in a cold, broken and lonely place, not of your own making and certainly not of your own choice, but sadly, here you are. This is your own valley experience. The backside of the mountain, the shadows, the fears. There is no way back, but the only way forward is just to be still and allow the process to move you.

"Whenever you find tears in your eyes, especially unexpected tears, it is well to pay the closest attention. They are not only telling the secret of who you are, but more often than not of the mystery of where you have come from and are summoning you to where you should go next."
Frederick Buechner, Whistling in the Dark

Although you might not need to hear it right now, brokenness, from whatever cause, is an antidote to pride. Why? Because it is the one tool which serves to break, mould and fashion our characters to the character of God more than anything else. To experience defeat, disappointment, loss—the raw ingredients of brokenness - all serves to move us closer to Christ being seen and witnessed in our lives more than glorious victory, gain and fulfilment ever can.

Oftentimes a poor broken-hearted one bends his knee,
but can only utter his wailing in the language of sighs and tears.
Oswald Chambers (1874-1917)

The tears of John, which were his liquid prayers, were so far as he was concerned,
the sacred keys by which the sealed book was opened. (Rev. 5:4)
Charles H. Spurgeon (1834-1892)

Mourning is a paradox. It is a painful yet at the same time, comforting, transforming and healing process, although we do not always see the benefits until long after. Sadly, some remain "stuck" in the process and are not able to move on; I pray this section will help release and remove the valve so the pent-up pressure can now escape, in Jesus name. Believe it or not, it's more painful and destructive **not** to mourn and far wiser to see brokenness as an ally than a foe. Many seasons of mourning have taught me that God delights to comfort and strengthen our faith, in the crucible of our greatest disappointments and sorrows.

The grief of great loss does not disappear.
Instead it becomes integrated into one's life as a painful part of a healthy whole.
Gerald Sittser

He Who Puts Together the Broken

"Come and see a Man who puts the broken back together again.
Again, yet I cannot believe you. But can you really find the pieces,
all those pieces that have been scattered over and trampled down,
buried in the deepest pits and darkest prisons;
scattered as far as the east is from the west?
Drop a glass and see; it is not only broken in pieces and scattered all over the place,
it goes into places you would never think to look.

What happened?
The identity of the glass is gone, broken into smithereens...
and like the glass you too cannot be recognised,
a sign that it's gone, and who can put you back together again?

The Potter sits and painstakingly gathers all the broken pieces of your life,
yes even the ones that are hard to find.
He lovingly begins to gather them together day by day,
week after week, month after month and year by year,
sifting through all the brokenness of your life.

Working through your pain and suffering,
your ups and downs, your tears of hunger,
rejection and nothingness of mind when there is no cry or voice,
when there is no one who can see or hear...
That Man can put you back together, although His body you cannot see,
His hand you do not know...
But His gentle breeze and the soft whisper of His voice
Will put you together again.

Margaret Dyer

Brokenness, Grief and Loss

As the last breath left your body, I held mine;
Eternity stood still as your life clock ran out of time.
I saw in that split second the essence of you and me
The past, present and now, no future, all came before me.

I held your hand and felt the temperature change as you moved on
I watched the sunlight grow stronger as I saw the light in your eyes was gone;
I stroked your skin and touched your face and knew you would never know
The pain I felt as losing you was your final, unintentional blow.

It's as if I'm in a waking dream and everyone else is asleep;
As if I'm aware of a secret so dreadful yet one which I have to keep.
No words, no song or tear can convey my brokenness, loss and grief
Yet I have to keep on keeping on, wading in muddy waters so deep.

I remember that moment as if it were yesterday
For although time has now sped and gone;
The pain of loving and losing you won't seem to release me
I feel I must bear my brokenness, grief and loss – alone....

Lisa Anthony-Rigsby

LIFE'S BEST & MEMORABLE MIRACLES

Come wrapped in brokenness, grief & loss

No heroics, no doing, nothing. For once, this action point is all about being still. Soul still, spirit still. Where you have previously been trying to get over the loss, where you have been trying to bury it so that you can carry on, just breath and be still. Let God take your hand and let Him guide you to a quiet place, your secret place, and minister to you as only He knows how. He is here to help and to heal, to comfort and to counsel and above all, to love you.... *"Be still and know that I am God."* Hold out your hand and let His comforting presence begin to cover you in the midst of your grief, loss and brokenness...

THERE ARE SOME HURTS
*Which only **God** can heal*

Oh God, it's too much, it's too for me to bear! Why, why, why? Why didn't you stop it? Why didn't you let them live? Why did they have to fire me, ME? Oh God! It hurts! The pain is too much for me! I don't even have the right words to use, so I'll let the language of my heart – my tears – whisper to You, what my mouth cannot say. Thank you, Father, thank You."

🕮 Help me, Lord, to sift through the broken pieces of my yesterdays and the shattered dreams and hopes for tomorrow. I feel so empty. I have watched each and every dream crumble before my very eyes. I'm numb with pain to the point that I can't even feel You. I simply do not feel the need for me to live any more. I can barely breathe in and out, because the pain and the memory it evokes, threatens to stifle, choke and smother me. Oh God! Where were You when it happened? Why didn't You step in and do something? Don't You love me anymore? Don't You love me?

He is despised and rejected by men, a Man of sorrows and acquainted with grief. And we hid, as it were, our faces from Him; He was despised, and we did not esteem Him. Surely He has borne our griefs and carried our sorrows; yet we esteemed Him stricken, smitten by God, and afflicted ...Yet it pleased the LORD to bruise Him; He has put Him to grief. When You make His soul an offering for sin, He shall see His seed, He shall prolong His days, And the pleasure of the LORD shall prosper in His hand. *Isaiah 53:34, 10*

- The sacrifices of God are a broken spirit; a broken and contrite heart, O God, you will not despise. *Psalm 51:17*
- Blessed are they that mourn: for they shall be comforted" *Matthew 5:4*
- But what things were gain to me, these I have counted loss for Christ. Yet indeed I also count all things loss for the excellence of the knowledge of Christ Jesus my Lord, for whom I have suffered the loss of all things, and count them as rubbish, that I may gain Christ. *Philippians 3:7-8*
- "Oh, that my grief were fully weighed, and my calamity laid with it on the scales ... But I would strengthen you with my mouth, and the comfort of my lips would relieve your grief. "Though I speak, my grief is not relieved; and if I remain silent, how am I eased? *Job 6:2 ,5-6*
- Have mercy on me, O Lord, for I am in trouble; my eye wastes away with grief, yes, my soul and my body! For my life is spent with grief, and my years with sighing; my strength fails because of my iniquity. *Psalm 31:9-10*
- Even in laughter the heart may sorrow, and the end of mirth may be grief. *Proverbs 14:13*
- Though He causes grief, yet He will show compassion according to the multitude of His mercies. *Lamentations 3:32*

Time to Touch: Brokenness, Grief & Loss

It was from a point of brokenness that the woman with the issue of blood pushed through the crowd to get her breakthrough. It was an accumulation of grief, loss and brokenness that caused her to throw caution to the wind and to face the baying of a cruel crowd. It was the desperation of a broken heart matched by the pain of a broken body which led her to face the unacceptance of a society who could not see past its laws, rules and regulations to reach out in love, understanding and acceptance.

Yet, facing all this and more, she dared to oppose even her worst enemy – herself – to push through and, with all the strength that her weak, faltering and failing faith could muster, she touched. She barely touched. She wasn't even sure if she had touched...but He knew. He recognised faith, pure faith, when it touched Him.

As you relive the brokenness of your past, the tears of your yesterdays and the dread of your tomorrow, use YOUR faith to touch Him, just like the woman with the issue of blood. Yes, even in your unbelief, your grief, loss, sorrow and pain – you can touch Him. He is able and willing to responds and minister to your deepest need to be made whole. You may not even believe He exists, but the fact you doubt, means there is a seed of faith buried deep within. Simply make the choice to release your seed of faith to touch Him – and let your restoration begin.

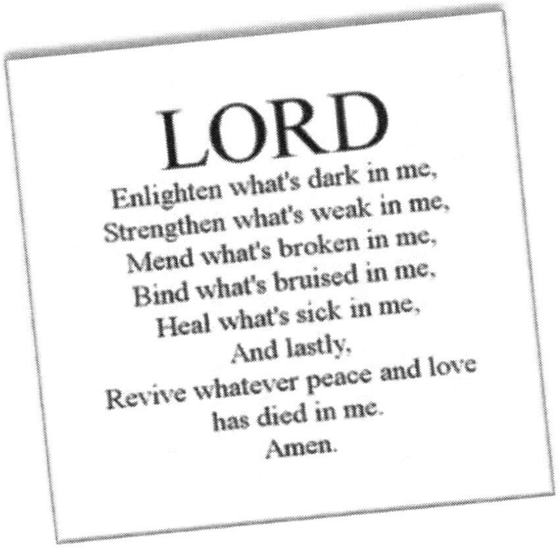
LORD
Enlighten what's dark in me,
Strengthen what's weak in me,
Mend what's broken in me,
Bind what's bruised in me,
Heal what's sick in me,
And lastly,
Revive whatever peace and love
has died in me.
Amen.

Go ahead & cry; it's just your heart speaking.
For tears are a language God understands

11 Health & Healing

The World Health Organisation (WHO) defines health as "*a state of complete physical, mental and social well-being and not merely the absence of disease or infirmity.*" (WHO 1948). The notion of health is nowadays seen from a more holistic approach, which was the intent of the original term, where the English word "health" comes from the Old English word ***hale***, meaning "wholeness, being whole, sound or well".

Determinants of health: The health of individual people and their communities are affected by a wide range of contributory factors. According to WHO, good or poor health is determined by environment and circumstances - what is happening and what has happened to people. In addition, WHO considers that the following factors probably have a much higher impact on our health:

- Where we live
- The state of our environment
- Genetics
- Our income
- Our education level
- Our relationship with friends and family

In essence, good health is not solely the absence of sickness and dis-ease, but more importantly, about being happy and feeling whole from a physical, mental and spiritual point of view.

Being healthy is not anymore just about taking medicines when unwell, it means taking care of ourselves to prevent any illnesses and to change our attitude when we need to heal or get better after the illness. Taking care of our health today means doing a lot of things to feel good, from eating the right way to taking vitamins, from exercising to having a job we enjoy. But what do you do when, in spite of all your best efforts – from organic eating to an annual gym pass – you are still knotted up inside with the stress of daily living? What do you do when your physical health is undermined by an overweight, undernourished inner self?

How many of us suffer from twisted intestines and turbulent tummy problems? What about persistent palpitations and horrid heart murmurs? When did we become enslaved to those time-saving gadgets which promised to free us so we could enjoy life – only to find that we are unable to plan one hour ahead without our mobiles / iPhones / laptops / kindles and whatever the latest social media gadget is out at the moment.

So, for all our health-supplement, pill-popping, organic eating, gym-attending, we are all looking for the next quick-fix health "one-size-fits-all" wonder drug! Tell me – since when did health and healing become so tiring..!?! As you ponder on this, I offer a disclaimer: unfortunately, this is NOT the elixir of life but a timely reminder of where and how to tap into the source of all healing and good health. Dear reader – it's time for your healing to begin! Read on for the beginning of what could well be, a complete health make-over!

Health Talk

One… Two… Three and rest!
One… Two… Three and rest!
Stretch and rise, stretch and rise
Relax, breathe and repeat three more times!

My morning exercises are a daily routine
To help me get fit, trim and lean!
Trying to shed extra weight hanging on me;
No more being unfit and unhealthy!

So up I jump and run on the spot,
Followed by torturous stretches, twists and turns
And I know it's working, for when I squat,
I feel the pain, as my muscles burn!

But on top of this, my soul is weighed down
With the worries and cares I carry around;
For when I worry about this or fret about that
My mid-section develops another layer of fat!

So no matter how many sit ups and crunches I do
The layers of fat just rolls with me too!
Until one day I realised, I need to exercise my mind,
I've got mental weight to take off and cast behind.

The mental exercise programme I'm now enrolled in
Is "Work Out for a Mean, Lean Skinny Mind-Trim!"
It's time for some real soul and spirit work-outs
Time to let go, let live and let flow!

To up my spiritual, love and forgiveness life pace
To do some stress checks and to monitor my score!
Cos it's not just the body that I've got to work out
But my inner mind health is what it's all about;

So it's one, two, three – stop, rest and breathe,
Gotta take it slow and sure, steady and easy.
For I now have to admit, even though I don't like it,
True health and healing has to start - within me!
Lisa Anthony-Rigsby

Oh, you're gonna love this! Get ready, here it comes:

- Stand up – straight! Shoulders back (the correct way is to lift them up, move them back and then drop them so your chest/diaphragm should be higher).
- Stomach in and hold it (helps to strengthen your inner core muscles).
- Stand with legs shoulder width apart and just look to the left – hold for a count of 5 (remembering to breathe deeply in and out for each count) and then repeat on the other side for a count of 5.
- With your arms at your sides, lift them up to shoulder height; point your hands as if you are trying to touch an invisible wall – stretch, stretch (yes, you can do it!) for a count of 5, then relax.
- Then, with your arms still outstretched, flex your hands upward, as if you are trying to push against the (same!) invisible wall – push hard for a count of 5 and then relax.
- In your standing position, clench your buttocks and leg muscles HARD for a count of 5 and then relax. (Feel free to repeat this as often as you like!).

Now, what's the point of all of that? Well, whatever your age, scientific evidence indicates that being even moderately physically active can help you lead a healthier life, by reducing many chronic diseases, such as heart disease, type 2 diabetes, stroke and even some cancers. Exercise helps to enhance and improve your self-esteem and sleep quality as well as increase energy levels. It can also reduce the risk of getting stress, depression, dementia and Alzheimer's disease. So, why not get active and take up the "one.. two…three and rest" challenge – today!

CHOOSE TO BE HAPPY

It's great for your health!

Father in this prayer, I humbly remind you of your word in *Exodus 15:26*, for you said that, *"If thou wilt diligently hearken to the voice of the LORD thy God, and wilt do that which is right in his sight, and wilt give ear to his commandments, and keep all his statutes, I will put none of these diseases upon thee, which I have brought upon the Egyptians: for I am the LORD that healeth thee."* Father, I am doing my best in obeying your commandment by grace, help me to trust you for healing. God remove this disease from me I pray in Jesus Mighty Name, Amen. Father, You say in Your Word that healing is the Children's bread. I desire this bread in Jesus Mighty Name, Amen. Let this healing prayer not be in vain in Jesus Mighty Name, Amen.

- Father, You say in *Exodus 23:24-25* that "*Thou shalt not bow down to their gods, nor serve them, nor do after their works: but thou shalt utterly overthrow them, and quite break down their images. And ye shall serve the LORD your God, and he shall bless thy bread, and thy water; and I will take sickness away from the midst of thee.*" Father, destroy all the idols in my life that I am consciously or unconsciously bowing to. Refresh my focus and my desire to serve you. Father you say that you will take away sickness from us, God, do it for me in Jesus Mighty Name, Amen.

- Father, You have written in Your Word "How God anointed Jesus of Nazareth with the Holy Ghost and with power: who went about doing good, and healing all that were oppressed of the devil; for God was with him." *Acts 10:38.* God please send an anointed servant to lay hands on me and let me recover in Jesus Mighty Name, Amen. Father, I curse the root cause of this disease and declare that your healing virtue flows through me in Jesus Powerful Name, Amen.

- I want to sleep and rest but my mind, Father, is ever active! Please release me from all those cares and worries which have gotten me so twisted and knotted up inside. Release me from the poison on an overactive mind. Let me put down all those things which I've been carrying and help me to get some sweet, healing sleep, because in You I put my trust and believe you will fix it all for me. For Your words are life and health to my flesh, sweetness to the soul and health to my bones. Help me to keep my heart with all diligence, for out of it flows the issues of my life. Give me a peaceful mind, so I can walk and live in perfect health, in accordance with Your will and Your word. This I ask in Jesus' name.

Behold, I will bring ... healing and medicine, and I will cure them and will reveal unto them the abundance of peace and truth. *Jeremiah 33:6*

- For I will restore health to you and heal you of your wounds,' says the LORD, 'because they called you an outcast saying: "This is Zion; No one seeks her." *Jeremiah 30:17*
- But to you who fear My name The Sun of Righteousness shall arise with healing in His wings; and you shall go out And grow fat like stall-fed calves. *Malachi 4:2*
- And Jesus went about all Galilee, teaching in their synagogues, preaching the gospel of the kingdom, and healing all kinds of sickness and all kinds of disease among the people. *Matthew 4:23*
- But when the multitudes knew it, they followed Him; and He received them and spoke to them about the kingdom of God, and healed those who had need of healing. *Luke 9:11*
- Bless (affectionately, gratefully praise) the Lord, O my soul, and forget not [one of] all His benefits, Who forgives [every one of] all your iniquities, Who heals [each one of] all your diseases, Who redeems your life from the pit and corruption, Who beautifies, dignifies, and crowns you with loving-kindness and tender mercy! *Psalm 103:2-4 (Amplified)*

Time to Touch: Health & Healing

If you have a cut, you will apply a plaster; if you have a headache, you will take an aspirin; if you sprain your ankle, you use a support bandage... (You get the picture...)

> Believe that *"the Word that God speaks is alive and full of power [making it active, operative, energizing, and effective]; it is sharper than any two-edged sword, penetrating to the dividing line of the [breath of life (soul) and [the immortal] spirit, and of joints and marrow [of the deepest parts of our nature], exposing and sifting and analysing and judging the very thoughts and purposes of the heart (Hebrews 4:12 Amplified)"*

I challenge you to take God at His word! Apply the Word of God as you would a plaster to a wound or a bandage to a hurting limb. Just as you would need to change the plaster every couple of days until the wound is healed, so you need apply the word of God until you get your healing! I *dare* you to try God, for He said, not me but God, to *"...prove Me" (Malachi 3:10)*.

For He also promised that NO word of His will return to Him void (empty) but will *"...accomplish what I please and it shall prosper in the thing for which I sent it." (Isaiah 55:11).* Dear reader, take God at His word and let your healing begin!

Heal the Past to Live the Present & Dream your Future

12 Relationships

Relationships are the glue, the ties, and the bonds which unite and keep us together. They define who we are, where we come from and, possibly, where we are going. They are the invisible threads and ties which help to keep us from unravelling – yet they have the ability to also leave us tied up in knots! Generic definitions of the term "relationships" include:

1. a connection, association, or involvement.
2. connection between persons by blood or marriage.
3. an emotional or other connection between people: *the relationship between teachers and students.*
4. a sexual involvement; affair.

Interestingly enough, the term "relationship" does not just include "*blood relations*", but also those with whom you have a "*connection, an association or an involvement*". This can be summed up in the old saying "*birds of a feather flock together*". Why? Because they have something in common – so take time to think about who you are "flocking" with. (This is a good place for some personal inventory!) If you realise the people around you have a tendency to gossip, back-bite and always love the latest scandal – oh dear! You could be "flocking" with such types because, whether you admit it or not, there's an obvious, albeit subconscious connection, association or involvement, which indicates you like the same things they like – and there's no denying it, either!

Think about it: how come all the gossipers tend to find and mix and blend with each other? How come all the grumblers and complainers get along so well? You turn up with your cheery self and you *know* you don't fit in! Why do all single women cling together (whilst the married women wish they could join the club once more?) Seriously, take a moment to critique (not criticise – critique) the calibre of those you are connected to, on any level. You will be surprised.

However, if you "hang out" with those who are honest and who have a natural zest for life. Those who are caring, generous and compassionate, that is a good indication of who and what you are. As another old but true proverb states, "*Show me your friends and I'll show you who you are*". Ouch! Let's hope the inventory of your friends, your associations and connections reveal what you are hoping to see.

So whether blood relations or soul-relationships – the latter being where you meet someone and instantly "connect" on a deeper lever – the truth is, we cannot survive without relationships. And that includes the bad ones, as they help us to appreciate and be thankful for the good relationships we do have! As you dip into your personal treasure chest of relationships, take the opportunity to personally thank those who are an integral part of your life. Recognise the residue of love they have left in, and on, you. Recognise the fragrance of their experience and the melody of their words and breathe a sigh of thanks for each and every one of them...

However, if you find some relationships are no longer a reflection of where you are and who you have become, this is also a good place to stop and evaluate – and see decide what action, if any, needs to be done. Whatever you choose to do, take the opportunity to view your own reflection in the reflection of the relationships around you – and may you also recognise the impact *you* also have on the lives and experiences of others.

A GOOD RELATIONSHIP

Will make you better not bitter

A GREAT RELATIONSHIP

Will make you sweeter, not sweatier

Friendship is a Blessing

Friendship is a blessing
it's the best you have to share,
The talents and the wisdom,
the capacity to care...

It's being there to lend support,
Whatever needs arise,
It's making sure that others know
They're special in your eyes...

Friendship is a blessing,
and, to all who have a friend,
It's one of the most precious gifts
that life could ever send.
Nathalie Byer

Heart prints

Whatever our hands touch - We leave fingerprints!
On walls, on furniture, on doorknobs, dishes, books.
There's no escape.
As we touch we leave our identity.

Oh God, wherever I go today help me leave heart prints!
Heart prints of compassion, of understanding and love.
Heart prints of kindness, and genuine concern.
May my heart touch a lonely neighbour,
Or a runaway daughter,
Or an anxious mother,
Or perhaps an aged grandfather.

Lord, send me out today to leave heart prints.
And if someone should say "I felt your touch,"
May that one sense YOUR LOVE
Touching through ME.
Nathalie Byer

Get a piece of paper and draw a circle (that's you) Next, draw lines from the circle and write the names of people you currently have "a relationship" with. Start with family and friends. Next, add work colleagues, next-door neighbours, casual acquaintances, even the newspaper agent you smile at when you pick up your daily paper. You will be surprised at the amount of people you know – and whose lives you touch.

Never forget:

*Who you touch is also touching **you.***

Father, there are so many people whose lives interact and intertwine with mine. Let me be a channel of Your blessing and love so that they may know You and Lord, may only Your goodness flow into me through them. I choose to give and receive only goodness and love. May all my relationships help me to be a better person – and may I have the same effect on those I come into contact with. Above all, may my relationship with You grow beyond my wildest dreams! May I have a true connection, association and involvement with You, so all I meet, may be touched by the sweetness of Who You are. Thank you, Father, Amen!

GREAT RELATIONSHIPS
Are always unexpected ones!

In your relationships with one another, have the same mindset as Christ Jesus. *Philippians 2:5*

- 🕮 Drink waters out of your own cistern [of a pure marriage relationship], and fresh running waters out of your own well. *Proverbs 5:15*
- 🕮 Even so consider yourselves also dead to sin and your relation to it broken, but alive to God [living in unbroken fellowship with Him] in Christ Jesus. *Romans 6:11*
- 🕮 Behave yourselves wisely [living prudently and with discretion] in your relations with those of the outside world (the non-Christians), making the very most of the time and seizing (buying up) the opportunity. *Colossians 4:5*
- 🕮 For the sake of my family and friends, I will say, "Peace be within you." *Psalm 122:8*
- 🕮 A friend loves at all times, and a brother is born for a time of adversity. *Proverbs 17:17*
- 🕮 Perfume and incense bring joy to the heart, and the pleasantness of a friend springs from their heartfelt advice. *Proverbs 27:9*

Time to Touch: Relationships

Everyone in your life is there, or has been there, for a reason: a divine reason! The reciprocal nature of your relationships has been divinely engineered for you to reach out and cry out to God – as well as for you to be a channel, through whom God can pour out His love into the lives of others. Take the time to think about the friend who was there for you. The one who gave you a shoulder to cry on. The one who gave you their hand to hold when you needed it the most. Remember the stranger who, or so miraculously so it seemed, rescued you from *that* situation - the one you thought you would never survive. In fact, remember the brother, sister, mother, father, friend – whoever it was - who loved you in spite of what you had done. For it was through that person, that God Himself was speaking to you, touching you and ministering to you.

So as you remember, simply use that memory to reach out in faith to touch the hem of His garment. He is the One who created relationships and is Himself, relational. Ask Him to minister to you through the love of those He has placed around you. And may you seek to be a carrier of His love and grace in the lives of others.

Relationships are always better, when we look to God!

13 Love

Be still my beating heart! The sound of love is in the air, the return of romance is here. Love. The very mention of that word can make even the hardest heart skip a beat and the fervent lover breathe a sigh of yearning relief!

There's no doubt in my mind that love, real love, principled and committed love, is the elixir of life. Songs have been sung about it. Books to numerous to count have been written about it. Poets and rappers alike wax lyrical about. And every day, we walk – or at least desire to – in the very atmosphere of love. If you are part of a family, then rest assured that, someone, somewhere loves you! (They may not *like* you, but hopefully, they'll love you – smile!) If you have a true friend, then that someone loves you! Even if you only have a cat or a dog, no fear! They are capable of offering unconditional love, even though you might have to give a stroke, a belly-rub or a plate of food but hey, it's still love!

Love is where the spiritual meets the natural because who can really explain the love of a mother for her new born babe; of a father who will work to ensure his family's needs are met? Who can explain the attraction of a man and a woman; ahh, the mystery of love indeed! Or even when you meet a stranger on holiday and you just "click" and know you have found a friend for life – someone you were able to just open up to in recognition of a kindred soul. However, in order to look forward in this section, we need to look back. The ancient Greeks had several meanings for the term "love" as follows:

- **Agape** (ἀγάπη agápē) means love in modern-day Greek and is from the Greek verb "agapo" – "I love". It implies a "pure," idealistic type of love, rather than the physical attraction as suggested by Eros and has also been translated as **"love of the soul."**

- **Eros** (ἔρως érōs) is the valentines' day kind of love! It is passionate with sensual desire and longing and comes from the Greek word "erota" which means "in love". The Greeks initially used to refer to feelings for a person, but which, in time, could grow into an appreciation of the beauty within that person, or even an appreciation of beauty itself. It is said that Eros helps the soul to recall the knowledge of beauty and contributes to an understanding of spiritual truth. Lovers and philosophers are all inspired to seek truth by eros. Some translations list it as "**love of the body**."

- **Philia** (φιλία philía), a dispassionate virtuous love, was a concept developed by Aristotle. It includes loyalty to friends, family, and community, and requires virtue, equality, and familiarity. Philia is motivated by practical reasons; one or both of the parties benefit from the relationship. It can also mean **"love of the mind."**

- **Storge** (στοργή storgē) is **natural affection**, like that felt by parents for offspring.

- **Xenia** (ξενία xenía), **hospitality**, was an extremely important practice in Ancient Greece. It was an almost ritualized friendship formed between a host and his guest, who could previously have been strangers. The host fed and provided quarters for the guest, who was expected to repay only with gratitude. The importance of this can be seen throughout Greek mythology—in particular, Homer's Iliad and Odyssey[1]

So, whichever "love" you are feeling and giving, rest assured, its source must be from the One from whom all true love flows...

*Never stop dreaming! Love **is** real*

[1] Source: The Four Greek Definitions of Love: http://www.naturalgame.com/showthread.php?t=7321

Love's Reassurance

To know you, is to love you.
To be loved by you is more than life itself!
What was meant to destroy me,
Confuse and annoy me,
The circumstances set to break me,
You caused them to make me.
I feel your love surrounding me, assuring me you care for me.
The clouds are gathered over me, the waves are high, they're drowning me.
But your still voice is calling me, repeatedly consoling me.

Alison Agard

I was asleep but my heart was awake...

I was asleep but my heart was awake...
It took Soul Mate – you, my mate,
To gently stir and awaken me
From my dream to a new reality
Where I can now exhale and start to breathe again...

I was asleep but my heart was awake...
But you alone heard my heart cry and saw my state.
So in your outstretched hand I've put my own,
And now I know, I **really** know,
That shadows do pass, for substance has come

I was asleep but my heart was awake...
And in your smile, your essence - my joy I now take!
For to me your heart you've given, a piece of heaven,
My entrance to love's gates, which have now reopened....

Yes, I was asleep, but my heart was awake...
And I now yearn for that time when our love, we can take
To sweet heights unknown, unseen, unsung...
For though I was sound asleep,
My heart felt your voice...my love, my one...

Lisa Anthony-Rigsby

Love Makes All the Difference

Love is the binding of two souls, hearts and minds
It is a sacrificing of one's self for another.
Love gives you the desire to hold on to that
which gives meaning to your life and
Helps you to make sense of life itself.

Love cannot be controlled or held back.
It reaches out, captures and changes.
It is like looking into the eyes of a child seeing everything for the first time
With excitement and without fear.

Love does not always need words.
It can be felt by a look, touch or smile.
It does not limit us; it allows us to be who we are and all that we can be.

Love is making a difference in someone else's life.
It is caring enough to see the good in others when no one else can be bothered.
It gives you strength too and courage to go that extra mile.
Love is the greatest gift anyone can give.

Sharing your love with someone helps you to make it through each day.
It is going through your trials, tribulations and coming out the conqueror.
It is knowing at the end of the day, you come home to the face of
The one you love – to find your smile reflecting back at you...

You know without a doubt nothing else matters because
You are in the place you were meant to be,
With the person you were meant to be....
Susan McCarthy

LET ALL YOU THINK & DO

Be thought, said & done in love

If you have ever felt unloved and unwanted, it is time to remove the lie and to live in the truth. With each heartbeat, you are loved; with each breath, you are wanted. With each sigh, you are cared for. And as you have freely received, so you are empowered and encouraged to give the love that beats in and through you. Determine to be a channel of love from this day on, as you reach out to touch the hem of His garment...

- Take a deep breath...and breathe again.
- Put your fingers on the inside of your wrist to locate your pulse, your heartbeat. As you feel each gentle throb, each fluttering beat, realise that what you feel is God's beat of love *in* you and *to* you.
- Now place your hand on your chest and *feel* your heart beat. That's love, His love within you. May the love you feel attract the love you need.

Help me to love like You. Help me to care, like You. Help me to feel, like You do. Help to understand, like You. Help to Love others.... Myself...and You. Plain and simple, help me to love. Amen.

There is no fear in love, but perfect love drives out fear, because fear expects punishment. The person who is afraid has not been made perfect in love. We love because God first loved us. *1 John 4: 18-19*

- You must not take revenge nor hold a grudge against any of your people; instead, you must love your neighbour as yourself; I am the Lord..... any immigrant who lives with you must be treated as if they were one of your citizens. You must love them as yourself, because you were immigrants in the land of Egypt; I am the Lord your God. *Leviticus 19:18 & 34*
- Love the Lord your God with all your heart, all your being, and all your strength. *Deuteronomy 6:5*
- You do well when you really fulfil the royal law found in scripture, love your neighbour as yourself. *James 2:8*
- Above all, show sincere love to each other, because love brings about the forgiveness of many sins. *1 Peter 4:8*

The Married Couple's Section

Dim the lights, take the phone off the hook and put a "Do-Not-Disturb" sign on the door. It's time to connect and reconnect with your spouse, your mate... your rib. Read a verse or two and just let your love do the talking...

She is a lovely deer, a graceful doe.
Let her breasts intoxicate you all the time; always be drunk on her love.
Proverbs 5:19

Come, let's drink deep of love until morning; let's savour our lovemaking. Proverbs 7:18

Stir, north wind, and come, south wind! Blow upon my garden; let its perfumes flow!
Let my love come to his garden; let him eat its luscious fruit! Song of Solomon 4:16

My love put his hand in through the latch hole, and my body ached for him. I rose; I went to open for my love, and my hands dripped myrrh, my fingers, liquid myrrh, over the handles of the lock. I went and opened for my love, but my love had turned, gone away. I nearly died when he turned away. I looked for him but couldn't find him. I called out to him, but he didn't answer me..... I place you under oath, daughters of Jerusalem: if you find my love, what should you tell him? That I'm weak with love.
Song of Solomon 5:4-6, 8

Set me as a seal over your heart, as a seal upon your arm, for love is as strong as death, passionate love unrelenting as the grave. Its darts are darts of fire— divine flame! Rushing waters can't quench love; rivers can't wash it away. If someone gave all his estate in exchange for love, he would be laughed to utter shame. Song of Solomon 8:6-7

His mouth is everything sweet, every bit of him desirable.
This is my love, this my dearest, daughters of Jerusalem!
Song of Solomon 5:16

Time to Touch: Love

It is written that *"... I have engraved you on the palm of My Hand"*.

At this point, take your index finger and gently trace each of the lines on the palm of your own hands. As you do this, realize you are tracing your own individuality and uniqueness. See each line as the very essence of who you are and realise that you are also engraved in the very palm of God. Know that each line is His love line, in, on and for your life. You don't have to pray, beg or seek for love. It is already written on your palm. When something is engraved, it means the item belongs to someone; it signifies ownership.

So when God says you are engraved on the palm of His hand, it means you belong to Him! Every time He moves His hand, it's a constant reminder of His love for you. He is crazy wild head over heels in love with you. Listen to what He says:

"I've never quit loving you and never will.
Expect love, love, and more love!" (Jeremiah 31:3)

From today, recognise that you are giving and receiving love, with every handshake you give. Let your handshake be a pressing through to the God of Love. Let His touch set you free. Your need for love will always get the attention of the ultimate Lover. All you have to do, is to reach out by faith, believe, touch and receive. Love has always been there waiting for you. It's your time to love and be loved.

May life give you a heart

to love you at your worst...

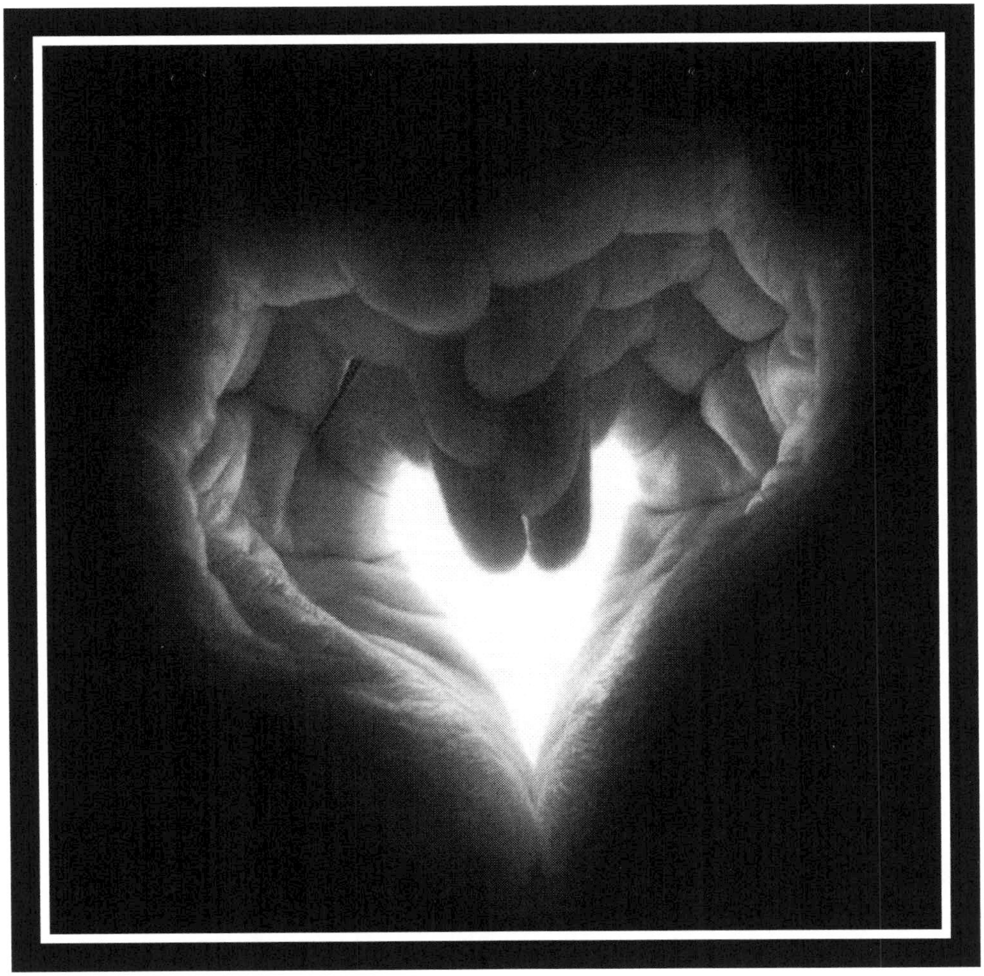

& arms to hold you at your weakest

14 Peace & Trust

Peace and **Trust** are related terms and like inseparable siblings, when you see one, you invariably see the other. They are the beautiful antidote to life's ugly sisters, Fear and Worry. These two masqueraders like to step in and make a bad situation worse – and that's when you will need Peace and Trust to come to the rescue!

Peace, as the younger sibling, evokes a delightful inner sense of tranquility and a feeling of being unburdened and light, without any weight. Peace is what a poor man can possess but a rich man cannot purchase. Peace is living above the here and now, above the cares of life, in a realm where the "there and then" is the reality here and now. It is like being in an airplane, soaring above the clouds of rain, pain and darkness, safe and secure. Now *that* is peace.

The Greatest Man who ever lived, promised His followers: *"...Peace I leave with you, My peace I give to you. Not as the world gives, give I unto you*". Indeed, one of His many titles is the "Prince of Peace". But where can you find peace in a crazy world? When everything and everyone around you is shaking, crumbling and falling away, where do you find peace, true peace?

Let me introduce you to its elder sibling, "**Trust**". Peace is the by-product or the welcome result of Trust. When you trust, I mean really trust, completely and implicitly trust, you can afford to be still and let go. When Trust comes, it reassures you by saying "hey, I am going to help you; don't worry, it's all under control!"

Some definitions of peace include an absence or cessation of war or hostility as well as a sense of safety, welfare and prosperity. When you are not at peace, you are, by the definition above, at war! Let's face it, the one person you are constantly at war with – is yourself! You battle in the dark recesses of your mind, the how, why and wherefores of your life. You struggle with the impossible task of trying to fit into a make-believe world of airbrushing and a perfect-10 presentation. You struggle to know if you're the only one feeling this way - even as you step into your designer shoes and get ready to face the external push and pull of another day.

You fight your desire to just get up and go; to just get up and run; to just get up and leave everything and everyone behind you. Yes, you are at war with yourself, within yourself and with the world. Every day. Yes, even now as you read this, you feel the struggle to just put it down, to turn the page and to forget that you even read this. Why? Because warfare is terrible, but when you are warring against yourself, that is even worse. You want to portray a picture of wholeness and peace but deep down inside, there's a battle raging behind the latest cosmetic application and the top-of-the-range designer fragrance.

Wait! Do not give up or lose hope! It is not all over. All is not lost. In the midst of all your turmoil and internal warring, there's a still small voice that, if you were still long enough, you'd be able to hear. It's the voice in each hot angry tear you have shed, in the raspy breathing of trying to catch your breath; it's the defibrillator which kicks in to give you a sharp shock to bring you round, when life throws you one curve-ball too many. Yes, it's is peace. Peace will surround you and zap you into a zone of safety, welfare where you can experience freedom from all strife and dissension.

So to get peace, you got to have trust. Trust in who or what you may ask? Trust in something, or Someone, outside of yourself. You know that, deep down in your heart, you cannot even really trust yourself. (Come on; how many diets have you tried – and failed? How many times did you promise, *yourself*, not to do this and that...only to find yourself in the same time and place?) No, it's time to trust Somebody bigger than you and I.

Definitions for Trust include:

1. Reliance on the integrity, strength, ability, surety, etc., of a person or thing; confidence.
2. Confident expectation of something; hope.
3. A person on whom or thing on which one relies: God is my trust.

You see, it's only by putting our trust in Someone outside of ourselves, we can experience peace. But we have to deposit our trust in someone who has been proved to be trustworthy, else we end up at square one – and even worse – as we'd be worrying now about whether He is indeed able to keep His word. Without a doubt, trust in Jesus is a guaranteed way of getting peace, real peace; a peace which the world cannot understand.

Trusting in Jesus for peace is what the woman with the issue of blood did. She had had no peace for many years, because she had trusted in her physicians, soothsayers and all sorts of medical mumbo-jumbo – as well as in herself trying this and that - to find the cure for her conditions.

Dear reader, where have you gone or are going to find peace for that which is troubling you? You have tried self-help but you're no better. You have tried the usual "remedies": sex, drugs and (as I like to say) a cheese roll – but you're still in turmoil, dis-ease and not at peace with yourself or the world. You have meditated, hummed, oohed and ahhed, but peace has been eluding you like a beautiful and ethereal butterfly. Today, you can receive peace, real peace, and everlasting peace.

How? By deciding to put your trust, in Jesus. By deciding to reach out and touch the hem of His garment. Because it is only when you decide that enough is enough, will you be able to let go... and let Him in. When the Prince of Peace comes in, oh boy, what a difference you will experience. Don't believe me? What have you got to lose, apart from war, hostility and inner turmoil.

TRUST GOD FOR PEACE

And with the pieces of your life!

Whisper Jesus

Today I got a burden,
And I felt that I should pray,
For God's spirit seemed to tell me,
That you were having a bad day.

I don't know just what that problem is,
But I sure do know the cure,
And if you'll only let Him,
God will keep you safe and secure.

In life there's always problems,
Cropping up to spoil our day,
But my friend, you know the answer,
All you have to do, is "PRAY."

If you still feel you're defeated,
And you want to run and hide,
Just reach out, and I'll be there,
Standing right there by your side.

So remember -- WHISPER JESUS,
For He's just a prayer away,
He's so close that you can touch Him,
All you have to do, is "pray".

Nathalie Byer

Crossroads

Sometimes we come to life's crossroads and
View what we think is the end,
But God has a much wider vision and
He knows it's only a bend –

The road will go on and get smoother,
And after we've stopped for a rest,
The path that lies hidden beyond us is
Often the part that is best.

So rest and relax and grow stronger
Let go and let God share your load,
And have faith in a brighter tomorrow
You've just come to a bend in the road.

Nathalie Byer

TRUST GOD FOR PEACE

And with the pieces of your life!

It's time to move from worry, stress and strife to peace and trust. It's time to stop, turnaround and begin to throw off what has been worrying and stressing you. It's time for you to raise your eyes above the parapet to see how and what you can and ought to be – worry and stress free! It's time to walk from this point on, in peace and trust, every single day of your life ~ and it begins NOW!

All I have seen teaches me to trust the Creator for all I have not seen

Father, I'm not really sure about all this peace and trust stuff; I mean, I've already tried it my way. Sure, I've had some successes but, if I'm truthful, there have been more misses than successes. I need a change. I need peace. I need to trust. I don't know how to do it, so I am here, asking You to do it for me. Please give me Your Peace and Your ability to trust. Thank you, Father.

✞ When I open the newspapers or turn on the radio or TV, everything around me screams war, disaster, dis-ease, breakdown and ruin! Where on earth can I even begin to look for peace? Indeed, how will I ever recognise it if I see it? I understand I need to be able to trust before I can find or experience the kind of peace I'm looking for. You say you can help me to have this peace. You say you can help me to have this kind of trust. Today, I ask You for a peace, which the world cannot give nor take away. Let Your peace still the raging waters in the reservoir of my mind. May your trust be my anchor in the midst of all emotional, mental and intellectual storms. Today, I hesitantly begin to put my trust in You with expectation that I will receive **Your** peace. Father, it's Your move now... Thank you, Father.

You will keep in perfect peace those whose minds are steadfast, because they trust in you. *Isaiah 26:3*

- In peace I will both lie down and sleep, for You, Lord, alone make me dwell in safety *and* confident trust. *Psalm 4:8*
- And the effect of righteousness will be peace [internal and external], and the result of righteousness will be quietness and confident trust forever. *Isaiah 32:17*
- And He said to her, Daughter, your faith (your trust and confidence in Me, springing from faith in God) has restored you to health. Go in (into) peace and be continually healed *and* freed from your [distressing bodily] disease. *Mark 5:34*
- Jesus answered him, Go in peace; your son will live! And the man put his trust in what Jesus said and started home. *John 4:50*
- May the God of hope fill you with all joy and peace as you trust in him, so that you may overflow with hope by the power of the Holy Spirit. *Romans 15:13*

Time to Touch: Peace & Trust

Just as the fingers on your hand are united yet are separate digits, so peace and trust are united, yet with individual functions and personalities. So today, right where you are (yes, even if you're on a train, plane or automobile!), link your little fingers or even cross your fingers together, to represent peace and trust coming together. As you link your fingers, imagine the intertwining of God's peace and trust joining them together. Be cognizant of the reality that, once joined, peace and trust cannot - and must not - be pulled apart. For when you have one piece of the equation, you automatically get the other piece in order to make up the whole

Let your sorrows, let your turmoil, your distress be the catalyst which propels you to reach out to touch the hem of His garment. For as your fingers entwine, see yourself faintly, oh so gently, touching His hem and know that a river of eternal peace and trust is now flowing *to* you, *in* you and *through* you. From today and for every day, know that you are at peace because you have chosen to walk in His trust.

15 Discipline

What is Discipline? When I think of discipline, I think of going to a gym, where a certain level and degree of discipline is needed to ensure the end results – increased strength and stamina – are achieved. However, for a lot of us, discipline is something we talk about, but seldom do! Like well-seasoned armchair coaches, we are always able to instruct others on how it should, could and needs to be done – without ever actually being in the game itself! I believe discipline is one of the main ingredients which takes us from hearing to *doing* and then from doing to *being*. Hence the term, human *being*. It's at this point we need to ask ourselves: in what areas do we need to discipline ourselves, so we can effectively, positively and proactively move from doing to ***being***?

Discipline also implies a sense of holding it together, stoicism, a stiff-upper lip, a firm stance in the face of adversity. A positive end result of discipline is the sense of inner strength, as having resolved to do a thing, you have strengthened yourself and find that you are now able to do bigger and better than originally anticipated. But to get there, you have to be determined in your ***mind*** – for that is where the battle is lost or won.

When you determine to do something, most people usually plan, have an internal picture, image or vision (call it what you like) about what it is they want to achieve. That is why, after the culinary explosion of Christmas with the resultant expanded girth, many join a gym, a local weight-loss class etc. We start out well, as we have an image of ourselves in our mind that we are determined to work towards. Sadly, the image begins to fade mid-January and by the end of February, the image has joined our other dreams on the sofa of life.

Discipline makes all the difference. Discipline is getting up when your body is screaming to stay in, sit down and be still. Discipline is when we by-pass our emotions and how we feel in order to achieve our goals, dreams and objectives; it is what takes us from here to there, from the chicken coop to flying with eagles! It involves training, rigorous self-training of your mind and emotions in order to fulfil your goal. It is a coach shouting encouragement to run one more lap and jump one more hurdle, just as you think your heart is going to burst and your legs give way.

Think of discipline as your personal, internal sergeant-major. Sticking to and working with the commands and directions it gives you, will help you achieve your goals. It especially likes to kick in when you think it's all over and are ready to give up.

It is the result of having faced – and come through – some of life's adverse situations and dire circumstances, where you've had to dig deep, deeper and deepest still, to draw strength and resolve from inner reserves you never knew you had. Discipline helps you to stand firm and face the brunt of the storm, with an inner determination not to fall or to fail. Discipline is here to give you enough faith and strength to take one...more...step. Discipline is not something you like, but you will be thankful for it, in the long run.

Yes dear friend, discipline is all of these – and more. In essence, it is one of God's life tools He uses to help mould, shape and file you into the special extraordinary and unique person, you are destined to be. So get with the programme – it will work out well with you.

*Discipline is the **bridge***

between goals & your accomplishment

Discipline

Discipline and training; correction and rules
Wow, it really grates my teeth!
Cos when I'm about to have another slice of cake
Discipline starts to speak!

It reminds me of my personal goals,
My dreams, desires and ambitions;
It tells me it's time for the gym
When I just wanna stay in the kitchen!

It reminds me to hold my tongue
When it's only half the story I've heard.
Cos discipline knows I'd be off to share
Each scandalous sentence...word by juicy word (hmmm!)

Discipline is what wakes me up
To drive me to my knees;
Cos it knows that when my good times end
It's to God I'm going to meet my needs.

Yes, it's my sergeant-major, my coach – my friend.
Discipline is willing to work with me to the end.
And when one day, its work in me is done
I'll be ready, fit and able to hear "Well done!"

Lisa Anthony-Rigsby

Left, right… left, right… left, right and attennnntion! **Halt**! Stand at ease. Sergeant-Major Discipline is in the house and it's time for YOU to get with the programme. For too long you have meant to, hoped to, wanted to, longed to…

Well, Discipline is going to ensure you DO! Sorry, it might mean a temporary end to some of life's luxuries and comforts. You will need your running shoes and tracksuit, as Sergeant-Major Discipline is now on YOUR case to get up, get out and get going! What is it that has kept you on the sidelines of life? It's time to get up and get back in the race. What is it that's kept you under the duvet of crushed dreams and unfulfilled hopes? It's time to throw them off, draw the curtains, open the window – and start to live again! What is it that's kept you stuck in the middle of life's highway?

Dear reader, Sergeant-Major Discipline is on your case! Time to get up, get up, get up… It's time for you to press through, determined and disciplined; your breakthrough is just a touch away…

I don't even have the desire to try, much less the discipline to succeed but I'm coming to You because I know I have a need. Father, as I struggle through the crowd of my own disappointments, my fears, doubts, insecurities and numerous other setbacks, I feel I am setting myself up to fail. I look to You to make the difference, to be the difference and to help me to stick with it, that thing, that goal or project you want or need to do. Father, I'm so used to reacting, I don't know how to try to put things in place. I need Your help right now, right here, so that I can be disciplined and determined enough to go all the way with You. Even as I push through the crowd to touch, may Your love push through to find and answer my heart's cry for a disciplined and steadfast life. Thank you.

✞ How many times do/will I have to struggle to take the next step? Father, I don't have what it takes to hang on much less to take the next step. I need Your help, right here, right now! Your word says that if we hunger and thirst, we will be filled. But what if we don't feel hungry even though we know we have to eat? I therefore ask you to touch my mental, emotional, physical and spiritual taste buds, so I can begin to move forward. Help me to be disciplined in order to fulfil the purpose and plans You have for me. Father, I need a touch right now…

Those who love discipline love knowledge, and those who hate correction are stupid. ***Proverbs 12:1***

- Don't you know that all the runners in the stadium run, but only one gets the prize? So run to win. Everyone who competes practices self-discipline in everything. The runners do this to get a crown of leaves that shrivel up and die, but we do it to receive a crown that never dies. *1 Corinthians 9:24-25*
- Know then in your heart that the Lord your God has been disciplining you just as a father disciplines his children. *Deuteronomy 8:5*
- I will be a father to him, and he will be a son to me. Whenever he does wrong, I will discipline him with a human rod, with blows from human beings. *2 Samuel 7:14*
- Yes, the Lord definitely disciplined me, but he didn't hand me over to death. *Psalm 118:18*
- Those who refuse discipline despise themselves, but those who listen to correction gain understanding. *Proverbs 15:32*
- But I discipline my body and bring it into subjection, lest, when I have preached to others, I myself should become disqualified. *1 Corinthians 9:27*

The difference between good & GREAT is

Discipline

Time to Touch: Discipline

The woman with the issue of blood was determined; she was disciplined. She could have thought about all the things that would, could and should have gone wrong, but she steeled herself to press through her internal fears and the external judgements and criticisms, to touch the Master. Why are you in need of a touch? Why is it that, every time you've tried, you seem to have fallen at the first hurdle? What is it that is keeping you from going forward and reaching higher?

As you read this, let the heat of determination and discipline rise up from your toes. Imagine it as a heat. Feel its flame starting within you, from your lowest point, rising up within you. Surely, it is time for you to take hold of life – your life – and to live it! It takes determination. It takes discipline. It's time for you to push your way through. Exercise your faith, for your breakthrough is a mere touch away. Discipline your faith. Push through – and win. He's waiting for you.

16 Education & Learning

Education and Learning are often viewed seen synonymously – but there are significant differences. **Education** is the formal process through which knowledge is acquired, whilst **Learning** involves implementing what we have been taught, whether in a specialised or generic field.

When considering the concepts of education and learning, most people automatically think of the school, college and university formula. It is where we have been "duped" into thinking that getting more degrees than a thermometer is what life all about. We force ourselves to fit an ever-changing curriculum, without ever asking ourselves if what we are learning is in line with God's plan for our lives. Please do not misunderstand me: there is nothing wrong with acquiring the HND, BA, BSc, MA, PhD and other letters of the alphabet after our name. But the bottom line is this: if we keep *studying* without ever *learning*, we will only be educated fools.

Our education did not begin when we took our first faltering steps as a 4- or 5-year old to on our first day at school. No, our true education began when we were in our mothers' wombs. Our initial education of the world outside the door of our mother's womb began whilst we were cocooned within the safe and protective waters surrounding us. We learned love or hate; we learned aggression or sympathy; we learned patience or impatience; learned to laugh or cry – all from within our mother's womb. Because what and who was carrying us was also teaching us through the curriculum of their emotions, experiences and lifestyle choices. Too many babies born with alcohol and drug dependency were sadly taught this from the classroom of their mother's womb.

So the our pre-birth introduction to Life Learning Module 101 is where we learned the moods, feelings, and thoughts of our Mothers - before we even knew what those things were! And on being born, our life education then continued in the rushing melee of our immediate society, as our working-Mums jumped from bedroom to baby room to boardroom in a twinkle of an eye – and then back again! No wonder most of us cried when we had to go to school for the first time!

In essence then, the concept of education and learning is more than just receiving a wall-full of certificates. No, our learning curve has been designated from the womb to the tomb. We never stop learning; and we dare to stop learning at our own peril! Every minute of every day is a learning experience – if we are able to see it as such. We ought and need to learn, not just from our mistakes but from the mistakes and life experiences of those around us. Many old proverbs we heard in our youth have revealed the wealth of their truth as we have progressed along our life journey. For example: "We will reap what we sow". Sadly, we also learn from our cultural media and advertising moguls, whose job is to teach us what to wear, how to look and what to say.

So this section is not only for those embarking on an academic journey but to all of us who are enrolled in the School of Life. Here, our learning started in the womb and the final class will end when we graduate to the tomb. In between each class, session, lecture and presentation, our experience will always have a practical application: in other words, have you been able to implement the lessons learned?

You will be challenged to recognise – and to thank – the most unlikely of teachers who cross your path. Look for the teacher when you hold the hand of a little child, in the smile of a stranger at a bus stop or on the train. It could be in the friendly and polite manner of a young person, or in the words of wisdom from an elderly neighbor or family member. Look for it in the eyes of your pet dog, whose wagging tail tells you it's just so happy to see you! Yes, life's teachers are all around – we all need to be open to see and to learn from them.

In doing so, you will also be encouraged to recognise *your* potential impact on others, as how you interact and react with those around you will invariably become part of their personal education and learning curriculum. We are all both teachers and learners at the same time. What an awesome responsibility!

So dear reader, please open your books. No talking. Class is ready to begin.

First Day at Work

Today is like my first day at school,
I'm shy, nervous, afraid and shaking!
Wondering if I'll remember each rule
Much less what class I'm supposed to be taking!

I stand outside the building;
Mum's hand is no longer holding mine.
I struggle with my new clothes
(And hope I'll grow into them, in time!)

I see so many people rushing past me
All looking as if they know where to go;
I've so many reasons why I'm dawdling and taking my time,
My feet are on a personal go-slow!

But no matter how I've lingered and stalled,
I've now reached the place I need to go;
So, taking a deep breath, I nervously enter in...
To start my first day as the company's new CEO!

Lisa Anthony-Rigsby

IT'S MORE THAN FACTS

Education trains the mind to think!

It's time to review our life curriculum, to see if we have implemented the lessons learned! In remembering previous circumstances, situations, mistakes and even that person, it's time to ask yourself what lesson(s) have been learned. So if you find your learning curve is comparable to a hamster wheel, use this section to get off, so you can start to get on with living a learning and teaching life! Remember: it's not just about what *you* can learn ~ it is also about what *you* have to teach!

Father, help me to be still so I can learn. I pray for a teachable spirit and a humble attitude. Help me to recognise the difference between knowledge and wisdom and for the strength to be able to implement them accordingly. Be my teacher. Remember I am a slow but willing learner – and even when I don't feel like, or don't think I can learn the lesson life has for me... please be patient, hold my hand and walk me through the education process of life, I ask in Jesus' name!

✞ Oh! Here I go again! I've been in this class before, have sat at the very same desk and even know the subject lesson! But why do I keep repeating the same mistake, having to retake the same class over and over again? Father, I'm tired of repeating and never learning! I'm tired of retaking but always failing! As I sit here at the same place with the same lesson book in front of me, I humbly ask Your guidance, strength and patience for me to get it! Father, I don't want to keep on flunking this lesson of life – so please help me! Thank you, Father.

✞ Help me to not just learn but to seek to teach; help me not only to gain knowledge but the necessary wisdom to know how to use what I have learned. Help me Father, to recognise that life is a never-ending cycle of learning and education; may I never stop learning! Educate me in those things that really matter; love, faith, hope, peace, patience and character. Help me to learn how to excel in them to the best of my ability, for Your honour and glory, amen

Father, I've embarked on this course (say what it is) and I'm struggling. I fear I can't and won't be able to make it! I doubt my ability to go forward and yet, I am too afraid and too advanced to go back. You said that if we lack wisdom – the ability to learn – to ask You. Well Father, here I am, in need of intellectual ability and know-how in order to pass well and excel. I don't just want to pass at the top of my class but I want to be able to retain the knowledge I am learning, so I can be a productive and proactive member of society. Father, I believe you have called me to study this course for a specific reason. I pray for the spirit of excellence, such as you gave to Daniel and his friends. I pray for spirit of discernment, such as the tribe of Issachar had. I pray for the ability to learn from all experiences, both good and bad, just as Joseph did. I thank you, Father, for giving me a mind of excellence, acceleration, acquisition and implementation and for the ability to learn and discern.

"The student is not above the teacher, nor a servant above his master ... It is enough for students to be like their teachers, and servants like their masters. Matthew 10:24-25

- Let the wise listen and add to their learning, and let the discerning get guidance. *Proverbs 1:5*
- Instruct the wise and they will be wiser still; teach the righteous and they will add to their learning. *Proverbs 9:9*
- I have seen something else under the sun: The race is not to the swift or the battle to the strong, nor does food come to the wise or wealth to the brilliant or favour to the learned; but time and chance happen to them all. *Ecclesiastes 9:11*
- But as for you, continue in what you have learned and have become convinced of, because you know those from whom you learned it. *2 Timothy 3:14*
- Jesus is God's own Son, but still he had to suffer before he could learn what it really means to obey God. *Hebrews 5:8 (CEV)*

Time to Touch: Education & Training

This chapter isn't just about formal education but also about daily lessons learned in the school of life! What exactly are you going through right now? Take a quick spot-check to see if it's something you have been through before but on a different level, in a different class, with a different teacher. If yes, it's time for you to graduate! In order to pass, you need to "touch the hem of the Master Teacher". For in doing so, you will (finally!) recognise the lessons you need to learn AND to pass, in order to move to the next class! I invite you to try the following:

- Close your eyes and imagine the situation and troubling scenario you are currently in and which you feel you will never get out off.
- Now, picture yourself in a huge auditorium, with a cheering crowd whooping and calling out YOUR name as you walk across the stage to collect your **Certificate of Having Passed with Flying Colours**! Visualise the colours, the sensations, the sounds and above all, your own feelings as you hold the proof of your success in your hand. Congratulations!
- Now, as you return to your seat, realise that what you thought you could NEVER PASS or EVER LET GO or MOVE ON FROM has just happened! You did it! You passed it! You let it go! You threw it out! You moved on! And above all, you have learned from it! Well done!

This is the moment to extend your faith to touch the Master's Hem and move on to your next level! He's waiting to help you take the next grade.

Learning will follows its owner everywhere.

17 Provision

A general rule of thumb definition of the noun "provision" is the action of providing or supplying something for use. In financial terms, a provision is an amount from profits that have been earmarked or set aside within the accounts to cover for any future estimated liabilities. Such financial "provision" enables the current year's balance to be more accurate and allows for a more efficient operational budget.

My personal definition is that provision is a supply or something that has been provided, prepared, stipulated &/or set apart for an anticipated future need. Therefore, in the world of work, a pension contribution payment is a "provision" against meeting future/anticipated expenses in old age. If we break up the word into "**pro**" and "**vision**", it indicates the necessity for us to have a "vision", before we can begin to prepare for it! Making provision for something you have no idea, need or anticipation of, would simply be a waste of time, effort and money! So, dear reader, what is it that you need **pro-vision** for? What is the vision you are seeking to provide for?

When we come to the Master, we come in our current, present situation, with no real prior knowledge of what the future holds. Yet we come in faith to seek an audience with the King for "pro-vision". We seek provision against sickness, unemployment, material, spiritual, emotional problems – even a broken nail! Seriously though, the provision God offers, is guaranteed to accomplish all we need – and so much more. When God makes an offer of provision, it is usually based on the "*plans that He has for us, plans for good, a hope and a future" (Jeremiah 29:11*).

So start thinking those areas for which you need provision, keeping in mind that, in order for your request to be heard and realised, you *must* have a VISION, a dream, an idea, a goal to which you are pressing towards.

This section is designed to make you stop and seriously consider what and where you want to be – and the kind of pro-vision that is needed. So forget where you are now... it's time to start planning for your glorious future, because, dear reader, you DO have a wonderful future ahead of you! It is NEVER too late to being planning, preparing (and believing) for it to happen.

Provision

I may not have - yet I am never in need
For I daily eat from divinely sown seed.
For Jehovah Jireh sees and hears my current and future pleas
And has lovingly provided for all my needs!

I have no wants, no burdens or cares
For all of these my Father is intimately aware;
Of those things I've needed, what I need and need still
So that I can live and walk in the path of His will.

To fulfil the purpose for which I was made
He is the pro for the vision for which I now seek;
His hands promise to provide
His heart is my refuge in which to hide.

Where I can safely rest in the promise He has given!
Divine provision on earth to last me till I get to heaven
Where, His glorious face at last I will see
My Saviour! My Provider! My ever loving Jehovah Jireh!

Lisa Anthony-Rigsby

Waiting On You Lord

I seek your face Father and I wait upon you,
For those who wait on you will renew their strength.
Thank You Father that you are my Provider.

There is not a need I have that you do not know.
For your thoughts are ever towards me and your banner of love covers me
I thank you Father for your word assures me "Let none that wait on
Thee be ashamed" My heart waits for you, Lord disappointment is impossible
With you. You are good unto them that waits for you.

Therefore I will look to the Lord, I will wait for God of my Salvation.
My Soul waits thou only upon God!
In the loving name of Jesus I pray, Amen.

Nathalie Byer

Get a pen and some paper and begin to write down your wildest dreams. I mean, those outrageous ones which you've hardly dared to express to yourself, much less tell anyone else! Now, next to each dream, put what YOU think you will need for them to be realised (remember: this is just for you, so be as daring and as bold as you like!) Once you've done it, put a line across it and write across on it, in big bold letters: "GOD WILL PROVIDE". You see, this is YOUR action plan which only the power of God can accomplish. So just give Him your list and leave it there.... Sorted!

WHEN GOD GIVES THE VISION

He will make the provision

Father God, I do not have nor do I know where to go to get what it is I don't know I need. That's why I have come to You. I don't know what the future holds nor where I am going – but I know need You to provide for me. I need divine provision for a vision I have yet to see and to realise! My life feels like it's in a rut. I seem to have been here, in this same space and place, for so long, I don't know if I *want* or even how to change. Yet Father God, I believe You see and know more than I do, so I simply ask You to provide what I need, for what lies ahead. I am trusting You and taking You at your word. Please, don't let me down. Thank you for divine vision and pro-vision. Amen.

IF YOU DON'T HAVE A VISION

You will always return to your past

....put (your) hope in God, who richly provides us with everything for our enjoyment. I Timothy 6:17

- And Abraham called the name of the place, The-Lord-Will-Provide (Jehovah Jireh); as it is said to this day, "In the Mount of the Lord it shall be provided." *Genesis 22:14*
- You visit the earth and water it, You greatly enrich it; the river of God is full of water; You provide their grain, For so You have prepared it. *Psalm 65:9*
- I will abundantly bless her provision; I will satisfy her poor with bread. *Psalm 132:15*
- And they all ate and were satisfied. And they gathered up seven [large provision] baskets full of the broken pieces that were left over. *Matthew 15:37*
- But put on the Lord Jesus Christ, and make no provision for the flesh, to fulfil its lusts. *Romans 13:14*
- But if anyone does not provide for his own, and especially for those of his household, he has denied the faith and is worse than an unbeliever. *1 Timothy 5:8*

Your future is like a diamond:

It may look rough, but just keep the vision & trust the process!

Time to Touch: Provision

It is time to stop trying to provide for yourself, and go to the One Who alone can give you everything you need, ~ I mean, truly need. Your bank accounts, credit, debit and store cards cannot help you. Your houses, cars, clothes, shoes, toys and all the other "stuff" of life cannot help you to provide for your goal and inner desire for a better, quieter and more loving you.

So, as you stretch your hand towards the Master, allow His virtue to pass from Himself to you and **be** the provision you need and have been searching for:

- Come to Him empty ~ and let Him fill you to overflowing;
- Come to Him empty ~ and let Him pour into you the very essence of life itself;
- Come to Him empty ~ and let the richness of His glory envelope you, not just for where you are, oh no, but a glorious guarantee of provision for your future.

Let the emptiness of your life be the touch that will get the Master's attention. Simply cry out and reach out to Him right now, right where you are.

All your needs are His desire. Your every longing is His need. Your every want, He's more than able to provide, He can and will feel your touch - and is ready to respond. All you need to do, is simply believe and get ready to receive. Provision is already yours.

THE PROVISION YOU SEEK

Is in the promise you have been given

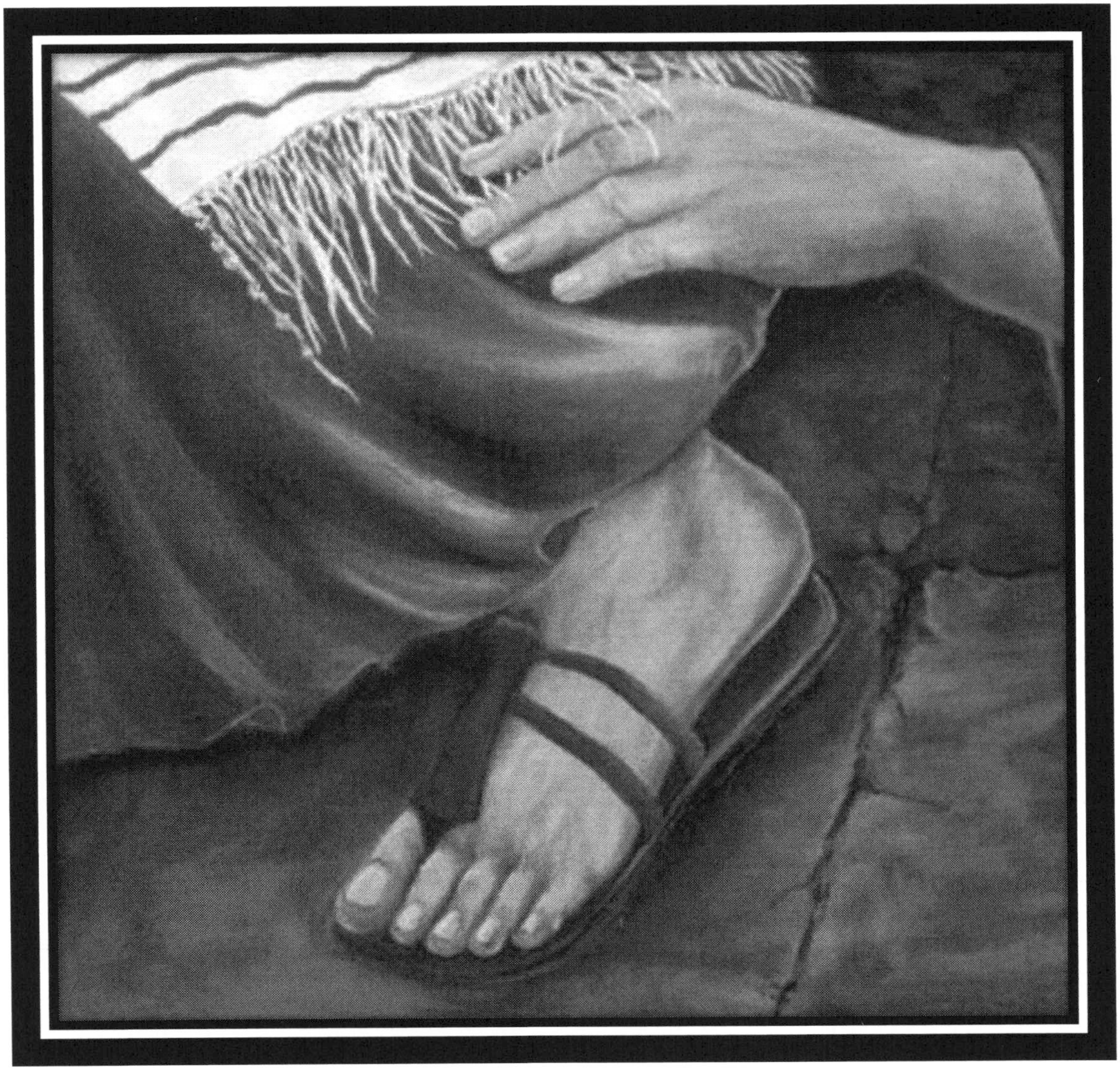

One touch of faith — and all your needs will be met.
Exercise your faith. Provision is waiting.

18 Strength

Now, what comes to mind – or at least *my* mind - when most people think about "strength", is usually a muscle-bound man, grunting and groaning, neck straining and eyes popping as he prepares to lift a mega weight. Such characters put in a lot of training to develop a distinctive "V" shape with the obligatory abdominal six-pack. Mythical characters that embody the epitome of strength include "Superman" "Captain Marvel", "Spiderman" "Bat Man" and even "Wonder Woman".

But have you ever wondered how these super-human, super-strong beings always seem to put their underwear over their tights/trousers? Even "Wonder Woman" swung into action in a glitzy, lingerie number… but I guess that's another story for another book! Seriously though… maybe the message they wanted to portray is that the use of their underwear on the outside was indicative of their strength on the inside. Let me explain.

The Free Online Dictionary[2] offers the following definitions of strength:

1. The state, property, or quality of being strong.
2. The power to resist attack; impregnability.
3. The power to resist strain or stress; durability.
4. The ability to maintain a moral or intellectual position firmly.
5. Capacity or potential for effective action: a show of strength.

A key word that jumps out is "power". Muscles can indicate certain degree of power but the real source of power and strength is from within. Now for a little technicality! The brain is the engine room, the driver behind all what we can (and cannot) do. If you go the gym 5 days a week but do not believe you are strong and gaining in strength, it's not your muscle mass but your brain messages to your muscle mass that determines your strength! If you study 5-6 hours a day and yet keep on seeing yourself as stupid, unintelligent and an educated dunce, it's all down to your brain and the messages you are sending yourself which reinforces the negative image.

---

[2] http://www.thefreedictionary.com/strength- cited September 2013

Strength is therefore more than muscle or even sheer determination. It's tapping into the hidden reserves we were born with and given at the dawn of time, at creation itself, to help us make it through. There are essentially **three** different kinds of strength which are applicable, not just to the physical, but, more importantly, for the holistic self:

Static strength	Explosive strength	Dynamic strength
This is used when you try to move an immoveable object, or carry a heavy object. There is no movement of the object. The muscles do not change length (**isometric contraction**)	Used when exerting a force in a short, fast burst, for example when throwing a ball or taking a long jump	Repeatedly applying force, over a long period. It's similar to the muscular endurance used when performing reps during weight training

Now, when you consider what you have been through, the obstacles you have overcome, the hurdles you have jumped, the mountains you have climbed, the rivers you have waded in and the seas you have swum through, surely you can see it was the different degrees and usages of strength that carried and propelled you! You might not be able to lift a car with one hand (or even two!) but you survived a broken friendship, you overcame oppression, suppression and depression.

You might not think you're strong enough to run a marathon but you carried you and your family through many a dark and uncertain seasons, not knowing what, how or where but you kept on keeping on. You outran the sickness which the medical profession and friends and family were certain would take you out.

You outlived the liars and haters and backbiters only for them to marvel at how you did it. You walked with your head held high in the midst of personal shame, blame and adversity. How did you do it? When your name was at the top of your company's redundancy list, you don't know how, but you didn't go down and you certainly didn't go under.

Sure, there have been many dark days and sleepless nights yet, it was in the weakness of your situation, where you found strength to go on. When your prayer was "just one more step Lord, just one more step", ***that*** is when you tapped into and used *static*, *explosive* and *dynamic* strength to keep on keeping on!

Why? Because the strength from the Creator is in your DNA! You are programmed to succeed and never to fail! You are destined to overcome. Tap into your inherent ***static*** strength to just keep on standing! Burst through closed doors, situations, circumstances with an ***explosive*** mindset of an over comer and let the dynamite "***dynamos***" strength of God take you to your next level.

You are far stronger than you ever imagined. If you don't believe me, then hear what God says: "*In your weakness, My strength is perfected*" (Romans 12:8).

So the next time you get ready for the world outside, make sure you put your inner strength on the outside and go, take control! Time to exercise your muscles of love and flex your biceps of faith and trust. You will make it!

WITH A NEW DAY COMES

New strength & new thoughts

The Fight's Still On

So, you thought you had me, with my back against the wall!
A New Year with yet more issues to make me want to cry, holler and bawl!
But life, let me tell you this: I'm standing solid, I'm standing strong!
So bring it on! Do your worst, cos the fight is still on!

Yes, I had my share of bad relationships and on-the-job woes
Some of which caused me to trip, stumble and stub my little toes!
But life, I don't think you know who you're really messing with;
So bring it on, the fight's still on – you're not dealing with a wimp!

So you thought you could corner and trap me with debt and credit crunch?
Please, don't make me laugh! I've had tougher things for my lunch!
I may look like I ain't got much going on for me right now
But you made a sad mistake, cos it's not me but YOU who's going to bow!

I ain't fighting cute cos this one war I gotta win!
What? You thought I wouldn't remember the way I came in?
Listen, I'm not a defeated victim – can't you see my victor's crown?
So take a swing and do your best – I've already won this fight that's going on!

So, to all who are fighting the same old same ol', and thinking, "why me"?
C'mon, fix up, toughen up and look life squarely in the eye and you'll soon see
You gotta stand tall, get into your fighting position, cos the fight is still on!
And don't you ever forget – all your battles are already won!

Lisa Anthony-Rigsby

WHEN YOU FALL SEVEN TIMES

Strength makes you stand up eight

Time for some ol' fashioned circuit training in order to get the brain thinking, the heart pumping and the blood flowing! Think about three main issues, problems, concerns you are facing right now. Imagine them in the centre of a room. Now, determine which stance you are going to take – whether ***static***[3], ***explosive***[4] or ***dynamic***[5] - it's time to use them to shift them out of your life forever! Move from one to the other, for a couple of circuits.

Remember to take a break after each circuit to reflect, drink some water (or a cuppa and some biscuits), wipe your face ... and then get right back on it! The purpose is for YOU to tap into your God-given strength reservoirs to beat, defeat and overcome what's ahead of you. So, 1, 2, 3 ... let's go!

Father I am weak but You are strong. I often feel like a wimp in the face of life's onslaughts but today, right now, I am coming to you for strength. Real strength. More than Superman or Wonder Woman. I need strength to cope just to get through today. I need strength to believe I can and will make it. I need strength to believe that yes, I am worth it. I need strength to stand in the face of sudden and certain defeat. I need strength, your strength, divine strength to hold my hand in the darkness of life and to guide and lead me to the next level. I cannot do it without you, so here I am, weak but willing. Thank You, Father.

Right! I've exercised patience and self-control; I've stood on silence and caution. I've cycled through many twists and turns of self-doubt and low self-esteem. I've bench pressed through broken relationships, redundancies and sickness. I've squatted more than my body weight of bills, debts and bankruptcy. But today, right now, right here... this is more than I can bear! It's the straw that's threatening to kill me. So I'm lying here, broken in mind, body, soul and spirit, with just barely enough strength to whisper to you... "Help me".

---

[3] ***Static*** *strength reminder: is resistance against a stationary load, e.g. holding up a heavy table in order to move a rug, or pushing against an equal force as in a rugby scrum.*
[4] ***Explosive*** *strength reminder: involves powerful, fast reactions e.g. like a sprinter who is quick of the starting block or even someone who has to jump/move quickly in order to avoid a car or cycle.*
[5] ***Dynamic*** *strength reminder: use your powerful 'isotonic' contractions (wooo!) to lift or move a load e.g. to when lifting a heavy trunk (or several bags of shopping) or lifting and moving a piano.*

The God of my strength, in whom I will trust; My shield and the horn of my salvation, My stronghold and my refuge ... God is my strength and power and He makes my way perfect ... For You have armed me with strength for the battle; You have subdued under me those who rose against me. *2 Samuel 22:3, 33 & 40.*

- The Lord is my strength and song, And He has become my salvation; He is my God, and I will praise Him; my father's God, and I will exalt Him. *Exodus 15:2*
- You shall love the Lord your God with all your heart, with all your soul, and with all your strength. *Deuteronomy 6:5*
- As your days, so shall your strength be. *Deuteronomy 33:25*
- Love the Lord your God with all your heart and with all your soul and with all your mind and with all your strength..... To love him with all your heart, with all your understanding and with all your strength, and to love your neighbour as yourself is more important than all burnt offerings and sacrifices." *Mark 12:30 & 33*
- I pray that out of his glorious riches he may strengthen you with power through his Spirit in your inner being. *Ephesians 3:16*
- I can do all this through him who gives me strength. *Philippians 4:13*
- I know your deeds. See, I have placed before you an open door that no one can shut. I know that you have little strength, yet you have kept my word and have not denied my name. *Revelation 3:8*

With The Pain
Comes Strength

Time to Touch: Strength

Like the woman who pushed through the crowds, you too have to push, and shove and press your way through, in order to get your breakthrough. Although classified weak, unclean and an outcast she did not let that stop her. Static, explosive and dynamic strength rose up in her and just when she thought she'd failed ... she touched! She connected! She made it! Jesus heard the emptiness of her cry and felt the weakness of her touch. He responded to the strength of the power and determination which drove her forward.

In reading this, you are probably feeling the weight of the doubts, the dilemmas, and the difficulties which have surrounded and pinned you down – and which are still pressing against you, even now. Yet, as you exercise your faith, your touch will brush the Master's hem – and you will receive your healing, your strength and renewal.

Come on – it's your time to draw strength and be strengthened when you simply touch the Hem of His Garment...

THE STORMS YOU FACE

Are equal to the strength within you

The weakness of your faith is the only strength you need to touch the Hem of His Garment.

19 Holy, Righteous, Glory & Worship!

This final chapter section, which is hopefully the beginning of your new-found prayer life and relationship with God, is designed to lift you out of where you are, to get a glimpse, a foresight and a taste of where God would have you to be! This is where you begin to take your eyes off the earthly to focus and re-focus on the eternal and lasting things of life. The topics will prayerfully open your eyes and your heart, to begin to want to desire the things of God, the very presence and essence of God Himself!

The primary purpose is to whet your spiritual appetite. The aim is for you to begin to yearn and long for a prayerful and intimate relationship with God, just as the deer yearns and longs for water, in a dry and thirsty land (see *Psalm 42:1*). Yes, come with us as we seek to touch the hem of His garment in worship, holiness, righteousness… so that the King of Glory will come to us!

The terms "**Holy**", "**Righteous**", "**Glory**" and "**Worship**" give a sense of lofty grandeur and awe. These are not common sounding words, but lyrics which (should) resonate in our very being. They belong to another realm, as they are the language of the heavenlies and the discourse of the spiritual. They bring a sense of awe, wonder, grandeur; they point to a higher and purer way of living and being.

With this in mind, the following outlines are designed so that, when we reach out to touch the hem of His garment, we do so with faith, understanding and an greater awareness of the majesty and awesomeness of the One to Whom we are reaching out. This is the essence and culmination of this prayer and devotional book. This is what it's all about. Like the woman who dared to exercise her faith to touch the hem of His garment and received an outpouring of His healing virtue into her situation, we too, can reach out and touch. For who knows what goodness we will receive from the One Who died and Who now lives, with open arms and heart, every ready to answer the cry and a touch from those who reach out to Him!

Holy

Relates to and is associated with God or a deity; sacred. It also implies an endowment of and an investment with the highest form of purity, devotedness and virtue. The pre-Christian old English meaning was something "that must be preserved whole or intact, that cannot be transgressed or violated"[6]. Synonyms include: 1.*blessed.* Holy, sacred, consecrated, hallowed imply possession of a sanctity that is the object of religious veneration.

Holy refers to the divine and to that which has its sanctity directly from God, or is connected with Him. E.g. "*Remember the Sabbath day to keep it holy*" (Exodus 20:8). Something that is deemed ***sacred***, which may sometimes be entitled to religious veneration, may have its sanctity from human authority, as in a sacred oath. Something that is ***consecrated*** is specially or formally dedicated to some religious use: a life consecrated to service. Something that is ***hallowed*** has been made holy by being worshipped, e.g. a hallowed shrine.

When you seek to be holy, means you have taken the choice to be set apart or separate from sin and evil. In other words, it's a conscientious decision to leave behind, let go and turn away from situations, circumstances and even people who can have a negative effect on your life. It's also interesting that, we are not called to *DO* holy, but to **BE** holy; and we can only ever achieve this, when we realise our need and are willing to go to the One from Whom holiness springs. As you reach out to Him, He will give you the very thing needed in order to come into His presence. What a loving God we serve!

I AM THE LORD
Who makes you holy.

[6] http://dictionary.reference.com

Righteous

Righteous or **righteousness**, implies a sense of uprightness and morality for someone who chooses to live and act in a moral way. It's for someone who is deemed live a virtuous lifestyle. Indeed, terms such as righteousness, virtue and morality are considered by many as outdated and old-fashioned term, yet are still very much relevant, and especially so, in today's post-millennium modern global culture. Mention these words and some will think they're the latest designer fragrance on the market. Oh dear! Righteous is a sense of right-doing and right-being. It's not accepting the extra change when the cashier has under-charged you. Righteous. It is pushing your neighbour's letters through their letter box – even though you know they are the ones leaving all their junk mail outside your door. Righteous. It is offering to make the teas and coffees – again – for your work colleagues, even though you don't drink either beverage! Yep, that's righteousness, right there!

But on a deeper level, righteousness is the outworking of an inner reality and love relationship with God. It really cannot be any other way, else it becomes corrupted and tainted, and operates as legalism at best and spiritual and moral nit-picking at worst! That is why *love* is an essential and pivotal key component of how to live, and to actually **be**, "righteous".

Other definitions and synonyms used in conjunction with the term righteous, include "good, honest, fair, and right"[7]. Sadly, these characteristics are rapidly on the decline in today's world. The question is: will you choose to live a righteous life? And if so, how? The only way is to humbly go to the One from Whom all righteous belongs. Let your need be the touch which will release righteousness – a desire for right living, thinking and being – into your very soul. You have nothing to lose and everything to gain.

THE RIGHTEOUS

Keep moving forward

---

[7] ibid

Now, the wonderful result of living and being holy and righteous has been reviewed, we turn our attention to **GLORY** and **WORSHIP**

[Now, let me just pause here for a moment. If you have ever wondered why we are called "human BEINGS" as opposed to "human DOINGS", it is because we were not created to just DO but to **BE**. Let me explain. God does not want us to DO love, but to BE love. Not to simply DO happiness but to BE happy; not to DO healthy but to BE healthy and so on. Indeed, why stop at seeking to DO wealthy i.e. to get, have and hold, when you can **BE** wealthy, especially when so many of us has what it takes to generate wealth-streams of income, happiness, etc. This last point is a chapter by itself – but I'm sure you get the picture!]

Untold wealth is available;
all it takes is just a touch of
faith...

Glory

Drum roll, maestro! The very term just makes you want to blast out Bach's 5th Symphony – or at least to play something that literally elevates you, the real you, the *spiritual* you, into the heavenlies and into a better space and frame of mind where you can mediate, relax and focus on the real issues of life, love and the universe! Well, I'm sure you know what comes next – yes, you got it – it's definition time!

1. It's a very great praise, honor, or distinction bestowed by common consent; renown: *to win glory on the field of battle.*
2. Something that is a source of honor, fame, or admiration; a distinguished ornament or an object of pride: *a sonnet that is one of the glories of English poetry.*
3. Adoring praise or worshipful thanksgiving: *Give glory to God.*
4. Resplendent beauty or magnificence: *the glory of autumn.*
5. A state of great splendor, magnificence, or prosperity.
6. A state of absolute happiness, gratification, contentment, etc.: *She was in her glory when her horse won the Derby.*
7. The splendor and bliss of heaven; heaven.
8. Ring, circle, or surrounding radiance of light represented about the head or the whole figure of a sacred person, as Christ or a saint; a halo, nimbus, or aureole.[8]

When we describe something as "glorious", it usually means not of this world. It denotes something that is other-worldly, belonging to and stemming from, the spiritual . It means it is something that has touched our spirits and caused us, albeit temporarily, to live, *really* live, above the dross of our present existence.

IF YOU CAN JUST BELIEVE

You will see the glory of God

[8] Dictionary.com, LLC. Copyright © 2012. All rights reserved.

Worship

After having touched and caught a glimpse of God's holiness, righteousness and glory, our only response is to praise and worship Him! As has been said, "praise is knocking the door to get God's attention; worship is our response when He opens!" It is where we conscientiously and involuntarily shift our eyes from ourselves to on Someone higher and worthier of our attention, our praise and our very being.

The most important aspect of worship is not our posture. Worship is not the diagnostics of our position, whether we kneel, stand or sit. Nor is it about our rhetoric, eloquence and effusiveness of our prayers and petitions. Rather, the essence of worship is our attitude, our motives; in short, it is about engaging our heart, mind, body, soul - over very heart – into the purity of worshiping God.

Worship further acknowledges that, even though we may not understand the process, we engage our WILL to adore, reverence and honour Him. Even though we may not like the outcome or are still awaiting a response to prayers made a long time ago – yet, because we believe His word that He always has our best interest at heart, we make a knowing decision to still CHOOSE to worship Him. Worship is being determined to hold God's hand – even when it feels like He's trying to pulling away from us and, on occasions, seems to have moved a million miles away.

So why do we hold on? Why do we take such a stance? Because of Calvary and the One Who died on the cross ~ that's why. Worship is lifting your hands to declare that, "*though He slay me, yet will I worship Him*", even as your tears silently fall. Worship is seeing your deepest desires and heartfelt dreams smash into smithereens on the rocks of life and having your hopes dashed and discarded, while heart declares *"...my times are in Your hands*". Worship is the getting *that* letter, *that* phone call, *that* visit which confirms the realisation of your worst nightmare, and yet you still whisper, *"...they that dwell in the secret place of the Most High shall abide under the shadow of His wings*".

Worship moves beyond the brilliant explosion of an exuberance of praise, into the darkness of a one-on-One intimate meeting, with God. It is a time of refining, of polishing, of fire. Because as you rest in, and on Him, in worship, the dynamics of the worship relationship means He then rests *in* and *on* you, to perfect what He has started in you.

God asks us to be holy, even as He is holy; to be righteous, even as He is righteous. Our response should be to wildly and boldly knock on heaven's door, in eager anticipation for more of Him – and then fall at His feet in love, wonder and worship when He opens the door of His heart to let us in...

WORSHIP IS SIMPLY
Giving God His breath back

My dear friend. It is time, *your* time, to press through the crowd of doubt, unbelief, mistrust, pain, fear, guilt, anxiety, stubbornness, rebellion, pressures, through all of whatever has been surrounding, stopping and hindering you in your life, to date. It is time, *your* time, to step out in faith. For your slightest move, can make all the difference. All it takes, is just one touch. Simply stretch, s.t.r.e.t.c.h and extend your faith. And when you think you can't make it, when you think it's all over; when you think He'll never notice, or listen, or even love you again... He will move in, just a little bit closer so you can touch Him, for that too, is His desire.

For when you manage to touch, even a mere touch of the Master's garment, all His virtue, His holiness, righteous, praise and worship will fill and overflow you. It's waiting for you. It's all there and is yours for the asking. All it takes, is a gentle touch of faith.

Divine Presence

Heavenly Father in this place
I felt your breath upon my face
Lead me, guide me
Anoint me I pray
I know you will never leave me
As this is what you say

Your warm embrace I felt so strong
It overwhelmed as I sang a song
Worshipping you, my knees felt week
And my body began to shake
The tears I could now stop

This Divine presence
I could feel all around
The Holy Spirit had come upon me
All I could do was cry and be
Holy was your presence
Holy was the ground
That first night in MOR was so profound
So tell everybody that God is real
Maxine

Overshadow Me, Holy Spirit!

Overshadow me, Holy Spirit
As I walk in and step out in purpose and destiny,
Overshadow; Come in to fill
And impregnate me with Holy Seed,
So what is within will be Holy and Righteous
and acceptable to Thee...

Overshadow me, Holy Spirit!
As I, in virgin circumstances and newness of mind,
Freely open my heart as You come and move me,
Into eternal destiny from this vision of limited time

Overshadow and come upon me, Holy Spirit!!
Fill my inner recesses, depths and hidden places
And I'll I wait, soul and spirit still, for Your purpose
To lead me to my destined, eternal space!

Overtake and overshadow me, Holy Spirit!
Hold and embrace me, and may our union
Fulfil the tenure of His prayer for us to be One...
Even as He and the Father are One...
Overshadow, fill and lead me, Holy Spirit
Lisa

Overshadow and fill me...
With Your Presence, Lord!

It's time to throw off your old, tattered garments of wrong living, bad doing and negative being. Time to dispose of your internal garbage of "stinking thinking". Time to flush out your old and sadly, familiar ways of doing and saying – and it is high time to tap into what God has in store for you. Believe that you can – and **must** - connect with the Master's touch.

It is time, your time, for you to fully experience His healing love and virtue and to let Him take you to a higher level. So, just reach up and reach out – the Master is waiting.

"Oh God! When I think about Your holiness, love and righteousness – the very purity of Your being, I shrink away in despair because I see myself as I am. But I thank God for the cross and, more importantly, the One Who died on the cross, because He saw - and sees me still - as a new creation, a restored and fresh revelation. I bow myself to you in praise and adoration, because who could ever love me so but You? My heart echoes the words of King David "What is man that you are mindful of him and the son of man that You even think about him?" Lord, I reach out to you in acknowledgement of the fact that You have been reaching out to me – and my answer is yes! Thank you!"

✞ "As I sit here in the silence of my heart and the security of my spirit, I worship You. The world is all around me but I choose to worship You. Situations and circumstances are threatening to overwhelm and engulf me, but oh God, I worship You! I consider the works of Your hands, both in nature - and in my own life, and how can I not worship You? Every breath I take is in acknowledgement of Your holiness, Your righteousness, Your majesty. I adore You, wildly and passionately, with every ounce of my being, for You are God and God alone. You are worthy, of all my praise, my worship – and my love. I worship You. Amen!"

Holy

I am the LORD your God; consecrate yourselves and be holy, because I am holy. Do not make yourselves unclean by any creature that moves along the ground. I am the LORD, who brought you up out of Egypt to be your God; therefore be holy, because I am holy. *Leviticus 11:44-45*

- Consecrate yourselves and be holy, because I am the LORD your God. *Leviticus 20:7*
- For this is what the high and exalted One says— he who lives forever, whose name is holy: "I live in a high and holy place, but also with the one who is contrite and lowly in spirit, to revive the spirit of the lowly and to revive the heart of the contrite. *Isaiah 57:15*
- For God did not call us to be impure, but to live a holy life. *1 Thessalonians 4:7*
- But just as he who called you is holy, so be holy in all you do; for it is written: "Be holy, because I am holy." *1 Peter 1:15-16*

And with that he breathed on them and said,

"Receive the Holy Spirit."

John 20:22

Righteous

Lead me, O LORD, in Your righteousness because of my enemies; make Your way straight before my face...for You, O LORD, will bless the righteous... and favour surround him as with a shield. Psalm 5:8 & 12

- And Abram believed in the LORD, and He accounted it to him for righteousness. *Genesis 15:6*
- He is the Rock, His work is perfect; for all His ways are justice, a God of truth and without injustice; righteous and upright is He. *Deuteronomy 32:4*
- Offer the sacrifices of righteousness, and put your trust in the LORD. *Psalm 4:5*
- The fear of the LORD is clean, enduring forever; the judgments of the LORD are true and righteous altogether. *Psalm 19:9*
- The eyes of the LORD are on the righteous, and His ears are open to their cry...The righteous cry out, and the LORD hears, and delivers them out of all their troubles....Many are the afflictions of the righteous, but the LORD delivers him out of them all...Evil shall slay the wicked, and those who hate the righteous shall be condemned. *Psalm 34:15-21*
- The LORD is far from the wicked, but He hears the prayer of the righteous. *Proverbs 15:29*
- But seek first the kingdom of God and His righteousness, and all these things shall be added to you. *Matthew 6:33*
- And I heard the angel of the waters saying: "You are righteous, O Lord, The One who is and who was and who is to be, because You have judged these things ... even so, Lord God Almighty, true and righteous are Your judgments." *Revelation 16:5 & 7*

He restores my soul & leads me in

His paths of righteousness

Psalm 23:3

Glory

The sight of the glory of the LORD was like a consuming fire on the top of the mountain in the eyes of the children of Israel ***Exodus 24:17***

- Glory in His holy name; let the hearts of those rejoice who seek the LORD! ... declare His glory among the nations, His wonders among all peoples ... give to the LORD, O families of the peoples, give to the LORD glory and strength. Give to the LORD the glory due His name; bring an offering, and come before Him. Oh, worship the LORD in the beauty of holiness! *1 Chronicles 16:10, 24, 28-29*
- But You, O LORD, are a shield for me, my glory and the One who lifts up my head. *Psalm 3:3*
- I am the LORD, that is My name and My glory I will not give to another nor My praise to carved images... Give glory to the LORD..! *Isaiah 42:8 & 12*
- So ... whatever you do, do ... all for the glory of God. *1 Corinthians 10:31*
- For our light and momentary troubles are achieving for us an eternal glory that far outweighs them all. *2 Corinthians 4:17*
- He said in a loud voice, "Fear God and give him glory, because the hour of his judgment has come. Worship him who made the heavens, the earth, the sea and the springs of water." Revelation 14:7
- Let us rejoice and be glad and give him glory! *Revelation 19:7*

*May God's glory be **your** story!*

Worship

God is spirit, and His worshipers must worship Him in the Spirit and in truth. John 4:24

- Why, my soul, are you downcast? Why so disturbed within me? Put your hope in God, for I will yet praise him, my Savior and my God. *Psalm 42:5*
- Worship the Lord your God, and his blessing will be on your food and water. *Exodus 23:25*
- Rather, worship the LORD your God; it is he who will deliver you from the hand of all your enemies. *2 Kings 17:39*
- Come, let us bow down in worship, let us kneel before the Lord our Maker. *Psalm 95:6*
- Worship the Lord in the splendor of his holiness; tremble before him, all the earth. *Psalm 96:9*
- All who worship images are put to shame, those who boast in idols— worship him, all you gods! *Psalm 97:7*
- Jesus said to him, "Away from me, Satan! For it is written: 'Worship the Lord your God, and serve him only.' *Matthew 4:10*
- From now on, brothers and sisters, if anything is excellent and if anything is admirable, focus your thoughts on these things: all that is true, all that is holy, all that is just, all that is pure, all that is lovely, and all that is worthy of praise. *Philippians 4:8*

Make **worship** *your weapon of choice!*

Oh, worship the Lord in the beauty of holiness!

Time to Touch: Holy, Righteous, Glory, Worship!

We've come to the end of this chapter and the devotional, but the experience does not have to end. Indeed, what is deemed the end of a thing could well be the beginning ~ *your* beginning! As you sit and bask in His presence, it is time to reach out, with that one ingredient guaranteed to get His attention – praise! Praise which pushes past the pain, the problem and reality of your present situation and circumstance, is guaranteed to propel you into His Presence!

So, for the last time, close your eyes and visualise your current problem, situation, circumstance. Focus on main thing which has been stressing you out, for so long. Picture whatever (or whoever!) has been stressing you out, as a huge bubble.

Now, with that image in mind, slowly lift your hands to shoulder height and pause. You are now in position to give up and finally release the problem. You see, whereas it had been too heavy and simply too much for you to deal with, by lifting your hands to praise and worship, you are strengthened to lift and get rid of it!! (Now, this is where things are going to seem a little strange...!)

Lift your hands above your head and open your hands wide, to release the problem. As you do so, then start to wave and shake your hands and (wait for it), to laugh! That's right, laugh! Laugh out loud and long! Laugh out hard and heavy! It's time to praise! Laugh out loud because you have given up and released the burdens and problems which were holding you back! Laugh out loud in the face of the enemy! Laugh out loud because, praise God, you are still here, in the land of the living! The devil could not stop you, the problems did not block you. All those negative issues designed make you trip, stumble and fall have now become your triumphs and testimonies, your stepping stones and your rise to favour!

Start to praise Him! Start to worship! Thank Him with a sincere heart for what He has done and is doing. You touched the hem of His garment, and if you are silent and still enough, you will feel His virtue, His love, His peace come into you – and your life will never be the same,

Reflection Section

Welcome to the MOR Touching the Hem of His Garment Reflection Section.

The poems are a personal reflection from those who, having reached out and touched, can now testify to how they have been changed. Each poem is a witness, to their tenacity and determination to get what they went for! For many, indeed for all, it was not easy – but they did not give up. They held on and pushed through their personal pains, dysfunction, perceptions and fears. One touch was all they needed. One touch was all it took. One touch was worth it all.

Today, they have each sown a poem as a seed to inspire you. Treat it as a poetry garden, with flowers and plants of different hues, colours, fragrances and textures, through which you can walk through, any time you desire. May the fragrance of their words encourage and embolden you to take your own step of faith, for your own breakthrough.

Shalisa

Walk of Faith

Your love O Lord reaches to the heavens.
Your faithfulness reaches to the skies glory!
I will speak of Your faithfulness and salvation.
I will sing of Your great love forever.

You are mighty O Lord and Your faithfulness surrounds me.
To proclaim Your love in the morning
and Your faithfulness at night is the desire of my heart.
I praise You, for You are the One who makes my faith to grow.

I ask You Lord, to help me stay in Your Word
so that my faith can grow.
I declare the entrance of Your Word into my life
that it produces growth and maturity.

I confess that if I live by faith and not by sight,
I daily confess what the Word of God
Says and believe it shall come to pass.
Lord, I ask that you will help me to hold on to
My confession of faith and to remember
faith comes from hearing the message.
Thank You Lord, for all things are possible through you
Amen.

Nathalie Byer

Footprints of Love

True love it comes and goes.
Making footprints on the soul and heart.
Securing paths through this world of woe.
Desperately struggling never to be apart..

Footprints of love make the heart stronger.
Fate causes others to drift far away.
Some passions linger a little bit longer.
Others return on a given special day..

Heart is a mansion love takes possession of.
Future promises that you would never forget.
Floating gracefully on the wings of a dove.
Always, forever loving without deepest regret.

Even love unreturned has it's rainbow.
A heart, that loves, stays forever young.
When you truly have loved with flow.
Love is only over when life is done..

Nathalie Byer

On the Wings of a Prayer

Just close your Eyes and open your heart,
And feel your worries and cares depart.
Just yield yourself to the Father above,
And let him hold you secure in his love.

For life on earth grows more involved,
With endless problems that can't be solved,
But God only ask us to do our best,
Then he will take over and finish the rest...

So when you are tired, discouraged and blue,
There is always one door that is open to you,
And that is the door to The House of Prayer,
And you'll find God waiting to meet you there.

And The House of Prayer is no further away,
Than the quiet spot where you kneel and pray.
For the heart is a temple when God is there
As we place ourselves in his loving care.

And he hears every prayer and answers each one
When we Pray in His name - Thy will be done.
The burdens that seemed too heavy to bear
Are lifted away on the wings of a prayer.

Nathalie Byer

God is my Strong Tower

Satan tried to take my life, that conference night
Whilst I was at MOR
It was called "Believe God and See"
When Satan tried to get a hold of me

Satan that foolish serpent
Went about it the wrong way
He forgot you see
That I am a child of the Most High
And the battle does not belong to me

That night I was singing and dancing
And praising God's Holy name
I am saved, sanctified and covered by the blood
I believe God and stand on His word
I am more than a conqueror
Protected by His shield
God is my strong tower
My refuge and strength

For what was meant for evil,
God reversed it for His good!
Healed and restored by love and mercy,
Simply believe God and see,
For I, am a living testimony.

Maxine Yearwood -Bailey

How Often We Wish for Another Chance

How often we wish for another chance
To make a fresh beginning.
A change to blot out our mistakes.
And change failure into winning.
And it does not take a special time
To make a brand-new start,
It only takes the deep desire
To try with all our heart,
To live a little better
And to always be forgiving,
To add a little sunshine
To the world in which we're living.
So never give up in despair
And think that you are through,
For there's always a tomorrow
And a chance to start anew.

Nathalie Byer

Friendship is a Blessing

Friendship is a blessing
it's the best you have to share,
The talents and the wisdom,
The capacity to care...
It's being there to lend support,
whatever needs arise,
It's making sure that others know
They're special in your eyes...
Friendship is a blessing,
and, to all who have a friend,
It's one of the most precious gifts
That life could ever send.

Nathalie Byer

No Footprints....

I've listened to the "footprints" poem
A million times or more.
Of how when only one set shows
Upon the sandy shore.
It is the Lord carrying us
And taking on our load.
And His are the only set
Of footprints that showed.

But what if when we look
There are no footprints to be found?
All we see is plain and simple
Sand upon the ground.
No imprints showing that our Lord
Is carrying us through life.
Helping us when we feel
We cannot handle all this strife.

Where is my Lord now that I've fallen
And can't seem to get back up?
So tired and lonely trying to deal
With what seems an overflowing cup?
Where are those footprints in the sand
To tell me He's right there?
Helping me with problems and
Showing that He really does care.

Does He have favourites, OH NO,
Please tell me that's not so!
By why does life seem easier
For some people that I know?
And sometimes I just scream out loud
although it seems in vain,
But often it gets harder each day
To deal with all this pain.

And then it dawned on me as I realize
How simple could it be?
I wonder why I was so blind
That I truly did not see.
It must have been a lightning bolt
that one day gave me light,
Cause out of the clear blue sky,
I finally regained my sight.

I saw a fluffy white cloud
Shaped like an Angel dear.
That helped me to understand
and see things oh so clear,
That when I saw no footprints
and so often wondered why,
My Lord carried me on Angel wings,
When He decided to fly.

Nathalie Byer

GOD'S FOOTPRINTS OF LOVE
Are right where you walk

A Friend Should Be Radical

A Friend should be radical,
They should love you
when you're unlovable,
Hug you when you're un-huggable,
And bear with you, when you're unbearable

A Friend should be fanatical;
They should cheer
when the whole world boos,
Dance when you get good news,
And cry when you cry too.

But most of all,
A friend should be mathematical,
They should multiply the joy,
Divide the sorrow,

Subtract the past,
And add to tomorrow,
Calculate the need
deep in your heart,
And always be bigger
Than the sum of all their parts.

Nathalie Byer

My Purpose

I want to fulfil my purpose
I want to fulfil the Plan!
I want to step into the Grant Design
To be the Best and all that I can!!

I want to reach for the highest start,
To reach beyond my wildest dreams;
I want to live above what the world says I am
Striving to be what I was created to be!

I want to be His Hands, His Feet,
His Heart of Love to the world around
Yes, I want to live my Father's dream
And leave the sordidness tying me to the ground.

Yes that's right, I want to fulfil my purpose
My dreams and desires to come true;
For ***I*** know I'm made with a plan to fulfil…
The real question now is… What about YOU?

Lisa Anthony-Rigsby

Friends we meet along the way
Helps us to appreciate the journey

Revival Night

The third night in MOR
The Church was on fire!
It was a night of revival
The Psalmist sang "I have confidence"
It brought the Church to their feet
The Holy Spirit was doing His thing
People were singing, dancing, holding hands
The place was on fire
It was a revival night
There were breakthroughs, healings and deliverances
As God came through

So hide yourself in the secret place
Bow your spirit as you seek His face.
Simply obey and trust in the Lord
He will always answer you with love and grace.

Keep yourself Holy and Righteous
And you will feel the Lord's touch
Maxine Yearwood-Bailey

You Will Never Walk Alone

I said, "The path is steep."
He said, "I'm at your side."
I said, "But I am weak."
He said, "For you I died."

I said, "Dark valleys come."
He said, "I'll guide you through."
I said, "But I'm not brave."
He said, "I'll walk with you."

I said, "Be light to me,
And strength as I go on."
He said, "I'm more. I'm love,
You'll never walk alone."
Nathalie Byer

The Fight's Still On!!!

So, you thought you had me,
with my back against the wall!
A New Year with yet more issues
to make me want to cry, holler and bawl!
But life, let me tell you this:
I'm standing solid, I'm standing strong!
So bring it on! Do your worst,
cos the fight is still on!

Yes, I had my share of bad relationships, situations and on-the-job woes
Some of which caused me to trip and fall,
to stumble and stub my little toes!
But life, I don't think you know exactly
who you're really messing with;
So bring it on, the fight's still on
you're not dealing with a wimp!

So you thought you could corner and trap me with debt and credit crunch?
Life, please don't make me laugh!
I've had tougher things for my lunch!
I may look like I ain't got much
going on for me right now
But you made a sad mistake, cos it's not me
but YOU who's going to bow!

I ain't fighting cute or pretty -
cos this one war I gotta win!
What? You thought I wouldn't remember the way I came in?
Listen, I'm not a defeated victim – can't you see my victor's crown?
So take a swing and do your best – I've already this fight that's going on!

So to all who are fighting life and thinking
"Why is this happening to me?"
Just be strong and toughen up
Be patient and soon you'll see
You gotta stand tall and get into position,
cos the fight's not over; it's still raging on!
And as you fight, never ever forget –
All your battles are already won!
Lisa Anthony-Rigsby

A Strong Woman vs. A Woman of Strength

A strong woman works out every day to keep her body in shape
But a Woman of Strength builds souls relationships to help her cope.

A strong woman says she's not afraid of anything..
But a Woman of Strength has God's courage in the midst of everything.

A strong woman won't let anyone get the best of her...
But a Woman of Strength knows giving is the best way God's love to share.

A strong woman makes mistakes and avoids the same in the future...
But a Woman of Strength realizes life's mistakes
are the keys to unexpected blessings
and knows who to turn to when uncertain and unsure;

A strong woman wears a look of confidence on her face...
But a Woman of Strength daily wears God's love, favour and grace.

A strong woman has faith that she is strong enough for the journey...
But a Woman of Strength has faith that it is in the journey
that she will become strong.
Anon

True friends show their love
In times of trouble, not happiness

Hello God

Hello God, I called tonight
To talk a little while...
I need a friend who'll listen
To my anxiety and trial.

You see, I can't quite make it
Through a day just on my own...
I need your love to guide me,
So I'll never feel alone.

I want to ask you please to keep,
My family safe and sound.
Come and fill their lives with confidence
For whatever fate they're bound.

Give me faith, Dear God, to face
Each hour throughout the day,
And not to worry over things
I can't change in any way.

I thank you God, for being home
And listening to my call.
For giving me such good advice
When I stumble and fall.

Your number, God, is the only one,
That answers every time.
I never get a busy signal,
Never had to pay a dime.

So thank you God for listening
To my troubles and my sorrow.
Good night, God, I love You, too,
And I'll call again tomorrow!
Nathalie Byer

Crossroads

Sometimes we come to life's crossroads and
View what we think is the end,
But God has a much wider vision and
He knows it's only a bend –

The road will go on and get smoother, and
After we've stopped for a rest,
The path that lies hidden beyond us is
Often the part that is best.

So rest and relax and grow stronger
Let go and let God share your load,
And have faith in a brighter tomorrow
You've just come to a bend in the road.
Nathalie Byer

Couple of Blessings

May your thoughts lead you often
to some quiet and restful place.

May you meet each new tomorrow
with a smile upon your face.

May you reach the star you aim for
and may your dreams all come true,

And where ever life takes you
may happiness always be with you.
Nathalie Byer

Butt Prints in the Sand

One night I had a wondrous dream,
One set of footprints there was seen,
The footprints of my precious Lord,
But mine were not along the shore.

But then some stranger prints appeared,
And I asked the Lord, "What have we here?"
Those prints are large and round and neat,
But Lord, they are too big for yours or my feet.

My child, He said in sombre tone,
For miles I carried you alone.
I challenged you to walk in faith,
But you refused and made me wait.

You disobeyed, you would not grow,
The walk of faith, you would not know.
So I got tired, I got fed up,
And there I dropped you, on your butt.

Because in life, there comes a time,
When one must fight and one must climb.
When one must rise and one must stand,
Or leave their butt prints in the sand.

Nathalie Byer

Time to Awake and Begin to Dream!

We have no excuse now, to slumber in the bed of our enemies' making;
To lie, death still, in the arms of mediocrity and complacency.
To snuggle under the duvet of demoralisation and dejection,
Plumping up the pillows of poverty, to get a good night's rest.

Time to throw off the cover sheets of want and lack,
To roll back satin covers of "*it'll never happen*" and "*no, no, not in my lifetime*!"
Time to kick out the hot water bottle of cold dreams, broken wishes and unfulfilled desires
And empty out its stagnant waters of "*no, can't do, cos that ain't for you*!"

Time to loose ourselves from the mattress of materialism
Thinking today's car and custom-made bling will, sweet soul rest bring;
Time to untie ourselves from the bedposts of boredom,
And stop leaning on the headboard of blame, shame and social security claims

Time to leave silk sheets of impossibility and cotton sheets of non-attainability,
To slip off the under-sheet of non-achievement with its matching cover of self-bereavement;
Time to turn over the mattress of woulda, coulda, shoulda, to let it air and let it breath…
It's time to wake up from sleeping, to open our eyes and begin to live - our dreams…

Lisa Anthony-Rigsby

An Awesome God

Wonderful Counsellor
Refuge and Strength
A friend you can rely on
Until the very end

Awesome and glorious
Faithful and true
My God will never forsake you.

Maxine Yearwood-Bailey

I Saw Jesus

I saw Jesus last week.
He was wearing blue jeans and an old shirt.
He was up at the church building;
He was alone and working hard.
For just a minute,
he looked a little like one of our members.
But it was Jesus - I could tell by his smile.

I saw Jesus last Sunday.
He was teaching a Bible class.
He didn't talk real loud or use long words,
But you could tell he believed what he said.
For just a minute,
he looked like my Sunday School teacher.
But it was Jesus - I could tell by his loving voice.

I saw Jesus yesterday.
He was at the hospital
visiting a friend who was sick.
They prayed together quietly.
For just a minute,
he looked like Brother Jones.
But it was Jesus - I could tell by the tears in his eyes.

I saw Jesus this morning.
He was in my kitchen
making my breakfast
and fixing me a special lunch.
For just a minute, he looked like my mom.
But it was Jesus - I could feel the love from his heart.

I see Jesus everywhere,
Taking food to the sick,
Welcoming others to his home,
Being friendly to a newcomer
and for just a minute, I think He's someone I know.
But it's always Jesus - I can tell by the way he serves.
May someone see Jesus in you today.
Nathalie Byer

Hello God

Hello God, I called tonight
To talk a little while...
I need a friend who'll listen
To my anxiety and trial.

You see, I can't quite make it
Through a day just on my own...
I need your love to guide me,
So I'll never feel alone.

I want to ask you please to keep,
My family safe and sound.
Come and fill their lives with confidence
For whatever fate they're bound.

Give me faith, Dear God, to face
Each hour throughout the day,
And not to worry over things
I can't change in any way.

I thank you God, for being home
And listening to my call.
For giving me such good advice
When I stumble and fall.

Your number, God, is the only one,
That answers every time.
I never get a busy signal,
Never had to pay a dime.

So thank you God for listening
To my troubles and my sorrow.
Good night, God, I love You, too,
And I'll call again tomorrow!

Nathalie Byer

Touching the Hem of His Garment

Just ahead of me, I see Him
Moving majestically through the hustling, bustling crowd.
My scent of sin and shame pervading me,
The silent stench shouting out loud.

"Unclean! Unclean!" echo the words in my mind
Words I've heard time after time
Yet, bravely I fight against their sound
For not in them, is my healing found.

I push past doubt and fear, pain and shame
Push past scornful looks and cruel, taunting names;
Push past my past of suffering and scorn
Push past my midnight tears and dry, dusty morns.

Push past society's culture and limitations
Push past religious mores and legalistic connotations;
I push past with every ounce of strength I have left
I have nothing to lose; my pride all gone, I'm alone and bereft.

It happened in a moment, in a twinkle of an eye
No one saw, it was a quicker than a sigh!
Yet, He stopped and turned and shouted, it seemed, in victory:
"Who was it? Where are you? For you have touched ME!

I felt virtue leave in answer to your faith
I felt pain give way to My saving Grace;
I felt peace leave Me to soothe your wounded soul;
When your brokenness touched Me, that's when you became whole!"

Trembling, I came and fell at His feet
Full of peace and joy; praise God, I was now complete!
One touch was all it took to get His attention
And it's all you need do, to change your situation!
So come, touch the hem of His garment, let His virtue flow through;
One touch is all you'll ever need to change you anew.

Lisa Anthony-Rigsby

Thank You!

The MOR Prayer and Devotional is designed to help you in your personal devotions and talks with God. The subject list is by no means comprehensive but serves to highlight some of the key areas which many of us may be struggling with.

It is our sincere desire that you will use this prayer and devotional book, to help you in your personal walk and talk with God – Whose Heart, Hands and Ears are ever open!

God bless!

Shalisa Anthony

add the

Ministry of Restoration International Pentecostal Church
London, UK

37419704R00085

Printed in Great Britain
by Amazon